Compass and Stars

Compass and Stars

MARTIN L. SMITH

SEABURY BOOKS
An imprint of Church Publishing Incorporated, New York

The essays in this book originally appeared in *Washington Window,* the
newspaper of the Episcopal Diocese of Washington.

Library of Congress Cataloging-in-Publication Data
Smith, Martin Lee.
Compass and stars / Martin L. Smith.
    p.   cm.
ISBN 978-1-59627-048-0 (pbk.)
1. Spiritual life—Christianity—Meditations. 2. Christian life—
Meditations. I. Title.

BV4501.3.S6527 2007
242—dc22   2006037523

Printed in the United States of America.

Church Publishing, Incorporated.
445 Fifth Avenue
New York, New York 10016

5   4   3   2   1

Dedicated to my partner
PAREE LAMONTE ROPER,
in love and gratitude

Contents

Acknowledgments

MY WARMEST THANKS are due to Jim Naughton, editor of *Washington Window*, the award-winning newspaper of the Episcopal Diocese of Washington, who invited me to contribute the "Bearings" column and has kindly permitted their publication in book form. And it has been a pleasure to prepare this book with the encouragement and expert advice of my friend and editor of many years, Cynthia Shattuck, and with Vicki Black, also a cherished friend and colleague.

I also wish to acknowledge the support and friendship I received at St. Thomas' Church, Washington, D.C., where I was a member for two years. In the last two years I have found a spiritual home at St. Columba's Church, and I am profoundly grateful for the privilege of serving this extraordinary and vibrant community.

Preface

THESE SHORT REFLECTIONS arose at a time when radical changes in my life brought the images of compass and stars to the forefront of my imagination. In 2001, after twenty-eight years on the monastic path, I took my leave of it for good, and found myself for the first time facing the challenge of finding my own way. No one was shaping my life for me: now to find my bearings, in a new life and a new city, with possibilities yet unknown.

Soon after I tentatively made a home of my own in Washington, D.C., I was asked to write a monthly column for the newspaper of the Washington Diocese. I proposed that we call the column "Bearings," to be faithful to the challenges I was facing myself. I also meant it as a sidelong reference to the compass rose, which is the symbol of the Anglican Communion. A fine symbol and a challenging one, since the Anglican way does not dictate rigidly preordained routes. It cherishes the skills that help us do our work of navigation, wherever we are, using prayer, imagination, and hard thinking to take our bearings in this constantly shifting world from the constellations mapped in scripture and tradition.

Becoming a householder, a taxpayer, a shopper, a cook; coming out; learning to be someone who danced and dated—all sorts of navigations are the background to these meditations on the interplay of the Spirit in everyday life. And then there was work. I decided to spend several years earning my living in a secular job, acting as a priest only in my spare time. Within hours of starting my job search, I was asked to join the staff of the United States Holocaust Memorial Museum as a writer. So most of the pieces collected here I wrote in my head as I walked to that wonderful and terrible place of dark pilgrimage, always conscious of the spiritual vortex I was about to reenter. Words are not strong enough to describe the disorientating force of the Holocaust, its brutal crushing of our moral landmarks and its caustic power to dissolve every religious certainty. Here was my daily thought as I made my way from my apartment, along the waterfront and past the fish market: How do I find my bearings with God today, in the face of *all that?*

It may seem frivolous, but I have often thought of the retort that Alice received when she complained to the Red Queen that she had lost her way: "I don't know what you mean by *your* way. All the ways about here belong to me." It seems a good enough definition of the mystical approach to religion, which understands that all life's ways, including the darkest, most winding or surprising paths, belong to the God who is One. These pieces claim to be no more than glimpses of how one man continues to explore that truth in his own life. But friends of all kinds who have been clipping them out, taping them to their refrigerator doors, copying them for friends, or reading them again online have wanted them to be put together as a book, so here they are.

Earth

1
Believing Bodies

I AM RUNNING out of shelf space for books in my little apartment and as I puzzled recently about which to keep I went into a reverie about the tiny collection of books we had at a home when I was a child. My parents were avid users of the public library, but owned only a couple of dozen books. I devoured them all from cover to cover. A self-help manual from the 1940s called *Relief from Nervous Tension* particularly fascinated me, since I felt tense and nervous a lot of the time. So at the age of ten I pored over it, laboring to understand the concept of neurosis and puzzling over the scenarios the author presented. One particular story made a deep impression. A patient who complained of chronic allergies entered his therapist's office only to be confronted by a huge bouquet of flowers on the desk. Immediately starting to wheeze and choke, the patient railed at the therapist for recklessly exposing him to such an irritant. Without a word, the therapist started to tear the flowers up. They were artificial paper flowers and entirely harmless.

Ever since, I have been fascinated by the power of the identities we create for ourselves. Who we think we are can dictate how the very cells of our bodies are going to react to the environment. The choking patient's body was obediently acting out his identity in the "allergic" reaction to what he assumed were real flowers, though in fact they were made of paper. Researchers have discovered that in patients suffering from multiple personality disorder, one of the personalities can be allergic to something while the other "self" isn't at all. One personality can be short-sighted and the other long-sighted, and the patient needs glasses with completely different prescriptions as she shifts from one identity to another.

Investigation into the ways our ideas get embedded into the very cellular structure of our bodies should be of paramount interest to thoughtful Christians. Our commitment to the mystery of Incarnation should make us especially alert to every source of insight about the way our beliefs affect us physically. All sorts of avenues should be explored more openly in our Christian practice as we build a richer understanding of what healing is.

Meditation and prayer are powerful ways of letting go of old identities and exploring new ones in Christ, and our bodies can register this change in a hundred ways, from the expression in our eyes to the ways we let go of stress. And transformation occurs through a flow in the other direction, too. We can allow our bodies to experience change first, and then a new sense of self can follow.

For example, there are many ways of exposing ourselves to deep healing of heart, mind, and soul through our bodies, through touch and movement. So, for example, it is a fact that our bodies act as the long-term "storage" for painful memories. This is not some New Age claptrap, but ageless human knowledge whose foundation is only now being investigated by science. Skilled body work—my experience has been with the technique called Rolfing—can release the pain and emotion embedded in particular areas of my body, freeing me to mature. Yoga and other forms of movement can be the royal road to a profound shift in the way we know and identify ourselves. I have been practicing *mudras* for some years, praying with a range of ancient gestures and postures for the arms and hands. I can't explain how these strange and beautiful gestures help shift my energies from petty obsessions, self-doubt, and negativity into a state of openness to God's presence in the present moment. I just know they do, and that I am benefiting from millennia of experimentation.

And what about the healing power of sacramental ritual? Our bodies can often offer us ways to grow into radically new identities of faith when our minds seem stuck in skepticism. I remember hearing of a Marxist intellectual in Russia who wanted to believe but could not overcome his agnosticism. He consulted a wise priest who strangely showed little interest in his visitor's intellectual difficulties with Christianity. The priest told him to go home and get into the habit of making the sign of the cross and bowing to the ground a hundred times a day in the privacy of his own room, then come back to see him when he felt like it. The man returned a month later and asked for baptism. First he practiced believing with his body, then his mind could catch up. There are thousands of men and women who find it hard to believe intellectually yet regularly take part in services in hospitable churches. Many are simply learning to believe with their bodies first. Through the rituals of worship the mental knots of their agnosticism are gradually being worked loose, and their hearts are being freed like a compass needle to align with the attraction of God.

2

Cookham Churchyard

I WILL ALWAYS remember a moment years ago, turning a corner in a stairwell of the Tate Gallery in London and confronting a painting by Sir Stanley Spencer called *Resurrection in Cookham Churchyard.* This huge canvas depicts with glorious earthiness and apparent naiveté the opening of the graves in the painter's local churchyard on the last day. The different generations buried there over the centuries are struggling up as if from long sleep and beginning to take stock of one another. In the middle there is a young man just emerging, looking to one side with a serene and serious expression—the artist's self-portrait. Back then, in the mid-sixties, the painting was regarded as dated and unfashionable and relegated to this relatively obscure place in a stairwell. There I stayed rooted on the stairs for over an hour, a young and troubled adolescent, anxious and struggling with depression I tried to keep secret, being moved to the very core of my being by the force of the resurrection gospel.

One of the best ways we can learn spiritually from one another is to share personal stories of the spiritual impact works of art have on us—the buildings, the music, the paintings, the sculptures in whose presence we have experienced epiphany, even conversion. In our western Protestant world, a culture dominated by thought and words, conversion experiences are often couched as events triggered by speech:

a preacher or perhaps an inner voice speaks to us and things change inside us. But our shared religious experience can tell us that symbols contain within themselves inexhaustible reserves of converting power, and we can be surprised by joy—and terror—and become suddenly sensitized to the grace of God when we open ourselves to them. Anglicans are sometimes mocked for their interest in the aesthetic, and we should be able to laugh at ourselves for what is often an exaggerated interest in good taste. And yet that laughter shouldn't shake our respect for something we know and love: the power of sacramental symbol and image to embody and communicate life-changing grace.

When we share our stories of religious experience, one of the most powerful themes that comes through is the uncanny way in which our religious experiences are timely. By coincidence—only it seems it never is mere coincidence—just when we need something so deeply, we turn a corner and encounter something that "speaks to our condition," as Quaker spirituality puts it. Somehow, when we are ready and not before, we have an encounter: the cathedral we happened to enter while traveling because we had an hour to kill before catching the train, the song that happened to be on the radio when we switched it on at random, the painting in the art gallery we would have missed if we hadn't obeyed the impulse to turn aside, the sculpture in the garden we wouldn't have had time to contemplate if our friend hadn't been delayed, the poem that stood out from the page when we were merely looking at books at random in the store to while away a moment.

Spirituality has a lot to do with gaining a sense that we have our own unique story about how God's grace has worked in our lives. These moments when God uses symbols and images to touch us can play as important a role as those grace-filled encounters with living people, the human angels who have come to us just at the right moment throughout our lives. And these grace-filled encounters have a double importance. They are not only milestones on the journey of conversion. They continue to yield new meanings as time goes on. Sometimes epiphany events are "a whisper which memory will warehouse as a shout." The original events can be fleeting, but over time our later experience brings them out in their fullness, just as the chemical bath in the darkroom develops the dim negative into a vivid picture.

The memory of my encounter with Spencer's masterpiece *Resurrection in Cookham Churchyard* is one I can visit again and again because the force of this strange and eccentric work of art never diminishes. When I first saw it, it didn't speak to me about the afterlife, but about *this* life, the life that lay ahead of me. I was touched with a sense of hope about my own creativity. And I wasn't surprised to learn that Spencer had started the painting immediately after his first sexual experience, because even at first sight, the picture challenged my ambivalence about sexuality and my uneasy relationship with my own body. Over the years, the painting has continued to bring blessings to me, and now in middle age, it keeps me company as I meditate on the future that awaits us in God beyond death. That future will not be the salvaging of a part of me, the soul, but the embrace of the whole of me, and in some way I will be even more fully an embodied person in eternity than I am now.

3

Jesus is a Jew

I AM OFTEN asked how the three years I worked on the staff of the United States Holocaust Memorial Museum have changed me as a priest. I can only answer, "In more ways than I yet realize." I am certainly more painfully aware than ever of the terrible consequences of the church's historic failure to fully embrace the Jewishness of Jesus. So when New Year's Day came round, I found myself regretting that the first of January is no longer celebrated as the Feast of the Circumcision, as it was in the original Calendar of the Book of Common Prayer. The change to calling it the Feast of the Holy Name must have seemed to make a great deal of sense in the 1970s when liturgical renewal was in full swing, and now only senior churchgoers remember the old commemoration. The very idea of holding up the fact of Jesus' circumcision has been relegated to a kind of religious attic where the church stores the obsolete.

Circumcision is that solemn act which marks every Jewish male with an indelible sign of his membership in the covenant people of God, and Luke faithfully records that Jesus himself was circumcised eight days after he was born. We know nothing about Jesus' personal appearance, but we can be certain about this physical sign of his Jewish identity. The old commemoration on New Year's Day was a reminder of that identity, and however sound the reasoning may have seemed for dropping it, the loss reminds us of a tragic dimension in Christian history.

"Tragic" seems overstated, but then working at the Holocaust Museum has forced me to stare day after day at those horrific events for which the groundwork was laid by the church's historic minimizing—or worse, virtual denial—of Jesus' Jewishness. Generation after generation was brought up to believe that Jesus was completely separated from the Jewish people, that Judaism was an alien culture whose survival was an obstinate hold-out against the new revelation of Christianity. The Holocaust could not have happened if the church had not been propagating for centuries an atrociously distorted theology that severed the connection between Jesus and his own people.

I used to imagine I was completely innocent of this attitude. After all, even as a boy, I could see through the bias in the depictions of Jesus as a blond Anglo-Saxon type in the stained glass windows. I made an intense study of the "historical Jesus" with scholars who rigorously emphasized Jesus as a prophet of his own people to his own people. My preaching was always grounded in the knowledge that Jesus was a Jew. But now I keep on discovering new levels of denial within myself. Not long ago the Presbyterian theologian Christopher Leighton, addressing a gathering at the Museum, jolted me by asserting that it is not enough for Christians to say that Jesus *was* a Jew; we have to say, Jesus *is* a Jew.

Leighton's words stung me into awareness. I realized that at some level I had been assuming that Jesus' identification with his own people in the covenant had somehow evaporated on the cross and in the grave. It was as though, in being raised from the dead, Jesus shed his Jewishness like a chrysalis and became a Universal Being and Presence. Paul's radical message that membership in God's community was open to all—"There is neither Jew or Greek. . . for all of you are one in Christ Jesus" (Gal. 3:28)—has had the unfortunate effect of seeming to make Jesus' inherent Jewishness disappear. I had never said to myself, "Jesus *is* a Jew"—let alone said in my prayers, "Jesus, you are a Jew."

Those who had the uncanny privilege of seeing the risen Christ described a body still bearing the wounds of crucifixion: "He showed them his hands and his side" (John 20:20). Just as surely Christ's body bore—we must say *bears*—the marks of the first wound that sealed him irrevocably with the sign of the covenant. And so perhaps there is a loss that can still be tragic, if we forget Jesus' circumcision.

Many are highly reluctant to meditate in this way. The prudish will recoil from alluding to Jesus' genitals; they need to keep anything sexual out of spirituality. Some feminists may have problems with such an overt reminder of Jesus' maleness; it may seem like a regression to an old spirituality that implied that males reflected God's image more than females. And for many, the effort even to imagine a risen Christ as anything other than a metaphor for a vague "spiritual presence" is too much. For them the Word might indeed have become flesh, but that only lasted for the thirty-three years or so of Jesus' earthly life.

These are neutering tendencies in our religion, and they have a disturbing relationship with the anti-Semitic biases that have disfigured Christianity. They were much on my mind at times when I walked through the Holocaust Museum on my own, praying silently to the Christ who, even as the Risen One, suffers until the end of time in and with all the suffering. Passing by these countless photographs of those who perished in the Holocaust—a mere fraction of the six million—I at least began to grasp that Christ is never more united with humanity than in his solidarity with his own Jewish sisters and brothers, those who are and always will be his own kin, those who have borne such unbearable things—many of them at the hands of those who claimed to be Christ's own.

4

Even After Death

I HAVE BEEN praying for a friend who was diagnosed just a few weeks ago with Hodgkin's lymphoma. Today I received news of his death and I find myself so full of gratitude that I belong to a church that encourages us to pray for the dead. What an amazing blessing it is to know that although we really have to work to let loved ones go when they die, we can still maintain an intimate connection with them through prayer. Through and in Christ, we can still go on expressing our love for the one we have temporarily lost. In the body of Christ, we are still united and love can go on flowing back and forth, carried along on the currents of the Holy Spirit.

Anglicans have not always enjoyed this freedom to pray for the dead. During the Reformation in the sixteenth century, the practice was stripped from the worship and practice of the Church of England. This was partly a reaction against the superstitious abuses associated with the medieval doctrine of purgatory. Purgatory was conceived as a place of banishment to which the dead were supposedly sentenced in order to receive any outstanding punishment for their sins—a sentence that intercessions for the dead, Masses offered on their behalf, and indulgences applied to their account were thought to reduce. And partly it was under the influence of rigid notions of predestination, the theory that

God had decreed in advance our fate in the life to come, a fate that no amount of prayers could possibly influence.

I remember being touched by a passage from the diaries of the great Victorian Evangelical social reformer, the Earl of Shaftesbury, writing after his wife's funeral, that from this day forward, to his utmost sorrow, he could never pray for her again. This was once the prevailing spirituality. The dead were assumed to be beyond the reach of prayer.

Prayer for the dead only started being practiced again on a large scale under the influence of the Tractarian renewal movement that sought to revive Anglican theology and worship by tapping the rich sacramental and mystical traditions of the early church. From the mid-nineteenth century onward Anglicans began to learn that praying for the dead did not stand or fall with the idea of purgatory. The theory that people are prepared for heaven by being first *separated* from the risen Christ in a "place" of suffering is absurd. The only way we could possibly be transformed after our death is through Christ continuing to hold us in his heart. Only in the heart of Christ (which is where we all are through our baptism) could the departed continue to be changed into his image from one degree of glory to another. We do not pray for the dead because they aren't (yet) united to Christ. We can pray for them because they *are*—and they are more grateful than ever to have the support of our love as they open themselves to an unfolding transformation. (God knows how radical the change is we will all need to undergo after death to be whole and true and free!)

What made prayer for the dead much more commonly accepted by Anglicans in worship, at least in England, was the horrific slaughter of World War I. The tidal waves of grief that engulfed the population from the massive death toll washed away a lot of the resistance to prayers for the dead. Eventually, when it came time to revise the Book of Common Prayer, prayer for the dead had been sufficiently normalized in our church for funeral services and eucharistic prayers to include prayer for the dead. I say normalized, but praying for the dead can have radical implications. Jesus told us to pray for our enemies. That must apply to praying for the dead. Once we start being radically inclusive, praying not only for our "loved ones" but for strangers, for suicide bombers, for the criminals we execute and their victims, for anyone and everyone, we open ourselves to a controversial and radical spirituality of inclusive hope. Prayer for *all* the departed implies the possibility that those who die with the hardest of hearts can be eventually melted in God's presence, with the help of the warmth of our faith too, and those who die utterly broken and abject might be made whole in heaven, with the help of even our tentative and wavering prayers of compassion. Prayer for all the dead is a radical act. It even has political implications. In the great national service of thanksgiving in St. Paul's Cathedral after the Falklands War, Archbishop Robert Runcie took the risk of including in the prayers for the fallen the Argentinean soldiers killed by British troops. Prime Minister Margaret Thatcher found this offensive and unpatriotic.

It is a deep consolation to pray for the dead, and to know that when I die I will have friends who will pray for me. In fact it could almost be a litmus test for true friendship, if both of us have no doubt that we will always pray for one another, even after death has separated us for a while.

5
Fingers of God

IF I AM HONEST about it, the term "social justice" sometimes makes me feel uneasy. Will people associate me with those who think the church should confine its attention to devotion and charity, and avoid getting directly involved in the civic and political arena? I don't want that mistake to happen. I believe that churches should be constantly forming alliances and partnerships with a wide variety of other groups and agencies, to act collectively to redress the numerous inequalities that disfigure our society, confront injustices, and strive for fair standards. No, my unease comes from a queasy suspicion that by sheer repetition of the phrase we risk enthroning *justice* as the primary motive for Christian outreach.

Justice is, of course, an ideal that is critical to the churches' capacity to form partnerships with other faith communities and secular bodies to pursue common goals for the health of our troubled societies and our endangered world. The church must be willing to use the language of common ground in its ministry in the social and political arena. But the ideal of justice is not adequate to express the core of Christian mission or the heart of its liberating message. While being ready to talk "justice" we must be still more fluent in talking "grace." The gospel is not only patently about more than justice; it is a searching critique of the adequacy of justice as an expression of God's will for humanity.

A bell went off recently as I turned the pages of an old notebook in which I had written down some quotations from one of Christianity's greatest mystics, Isaac the Syrian, a seventh-century contemplative and pastor living in what is now Iraq. In his *Mystical Treatises,* Isaac frequently goads his readers to question whether in the light of the radical teaching of the gospel we should even call God just, let alone make justice our primary religious ideal. Writing about Matthew's parable of the laborers in the vineyard, which tells how the owner paid those who had worked only a short time the same wages as those who had worked all day (20:1–16), Isaac says:

> And how can you call God just when you come to the passage about the laborer's wages? Where is God's "justice"? . . . Do not call God "just," for his justice is not made known in your affairs. . . . He is good, as He says, to the evil and the ungodly.

Isaac goes on to talk about God's mercy:

> Mercy and just judgment in one soul is like a man worshipping God and idols in the same house. Mercy is the opposite of just judgment. Just judgment is the equality of equal measures, for it gives to each as he deserves, without inclining to one side or another, or having respect of persons when it repays us. Mercy, however, is pity moved by grace and inclines to all in compassion; it does not requite him who deserves harsh treatment and it fills to overflowing him who deserves good. And if mercy is on the side of righteousness, then just judgment is on the side of evil. As grass and fire cannot stay together in the same house, so neither can just judgment and mercy remain in one soul.

Isaac vigorously contrasts two perspectives. One focuses on ensuring that people get what they deserve, awarding them what they are entitled to, defining what their rights are. It is about blind justice that metes out reward and punishment on principle. Another perspective is opened up by the good news of Jesus, showing us a vista in which God reaches out in compassion to each and to all, repairing broken relationships, restoring community, reweaving intimacy, inspiring fresh beginnings and new connections, drawing people into partnership, teaching them how to embrace the dreaded "other," making sisterhood out of enmity and brotherhood out of alienation. All this leaves far behind the human categories of rights, entitlements, and deserts. God goes out of the way—so far out that the Beloved One meets his end on a Roman cross, "taken out" as a dangerous criminal—to reach out for reconciliation.

Wherever the churches seem to lean heavily on a short-hand secular vocabulary of "social justice"—one that sometimes veers into a clunky political correctness that can provoke our skepticism or weariness—it is because we are avoiding the task of framing for ourselves a true gospel perspective. It is seldom appropriate for Christian groups to present our theology overtly when working with others in the public, environmental, political, and civic arenas to promote healthy social change, except when genuinely invited to do so. But it is essential for Christians to keep on exploring among ourselves what is the distinctive motive for Christian outreach. We need more theology for our outreach, which means exploring how it is that God is shown in Jesus to be reaching out—to whom, and why. Our call to outreach can't mean anything less than a call to act as fingers for *God's* reaching out to all.

6

There is Only Us

WHEN I FIRST came to Washington a few years ago and
told friends here that I had moved into an apartment in the
Shaw neighborhood, some of them would respond with a
slightly worried expression, qualified by an assurance that it
was an "up and coming" area. I found myself living closer to
the kind of daily violence that gets buried in the more
obscure pages of the newspaper. I have woken to the rattle
of automatic gunfire in the night. Coming round the corner
one dark night, I found a policeman on his knees wiping the
pavement in front of the liquor store. The body of a stabbing
victim was just being stowed away in the ambulance in the
background. Over the weeks it took for the bloodstains to
fade, I said a prayer for the victim each time I passed. But
who was this person to me? Our souls are not trained to
react much to the death of strangers. It is a different matter
when we know the sufferer.

Just recently in Washington there has been a rash of mur-
ders targeting transgendered folk. For most of us, strangers
don't get stranger than these. Most of us don't know and
don't want to know people who have changed their gender.
I got a jolt one morning, reading about the latest victim in
the newspaper. I recognized the photograph they printed
with the story. This was someone I had met by chance some
weeks before. She was a rather striking, statuesque figure

who happened to be in a bar when I was there with a group of friends. One of them, in a most charming way, asked her to dance and she obviously appreciated this gesture, which the old-fashioned word "courtly" describes exactly. I even wrote a poem about the incident the following day. Now as I put the newspaper down, I felt more than a passing revulsion triggered by the report of yet another grotesque murder. I found myself grieving her senseless and awful death. Just meeting her by chance had been enough to create a bond.

But I get the feeling that this distinction between who I know, who I don't know, who I don't want to know, would be in danger of collapsing if I really were a true believer in the gospel. The gospel tells us a secret—and this is mysterious, wonderful, and appalling all at the same time—that our estrangement from strangers is the product of illusion, false consciousness. In fact our lives have the same roots planted in the same ground: "one God and Father of all, who is above all and through all and in all" (Eph. 4:6). And Christ is not only the Heart of my heart—"It is no longer I who live, but it is Christ who lives in me" (Gal. 2:20)—he is also the one who lives incognito in every stranger: "I was hungry and you gave me food" (Matt. 25:35). And so, by faith, I already know everybody's true self.

There is only *us* in Christ, no "us and them." Often in our church we try to get at this reality by constantly reciting phrases about inclusiveness, but this remains on the level of mere jargon unless we face the brutal realism of the gospel about our need to be broken open. Jesus told us that in order to break through to the sense that in God we are all together as equals and to the discovery that estrangement is illusion, we have to break free from those loyalties that foster the false consciousness of *us and them*. He spoke about "hating" our parents and leaving home, with the family standing for all those communities—our class, nation, denomination, or whatever—that we use to define ourselves through the exclusion of outsiders. To talk glibly about inclusiveness without going into the cost of breaking the ties that literally bind is futile. We have to practice becoming dissidents within our own communities whenever the loyalty they expect from us involves "hating our enemies." Becoming practiced dissidents is not comfortable or easy. Jesus' family once came after him, convinced that he was out of his mind. We are not rebelling against our own communities, but taking a stand on our loyalty to God's one family that includes both them and those they want us to disdain or ignore as aliens.

Steady practice in this sacred disloyalty, this unplugging and extrication, and steady practice in experimenting with solidarity and connection—these are the everyday exercises of prayer. Intercession is powerful, especially when, instead of imagining that we are calling "down" blessings on people from a God "above," we realize that Jesus is already in the heart of friend or alien. It is he who is looking at us, making a bid for our love, through the eyes of every human being. The street is our best practice ground, and whenever we momentarily pray for strangers, such as the wounded brother who left his blood all over the pavement outside the liquor store and the policeman who was patiently mopping it up, we are simply activating the interconnectedness that already makes us one in God.

Vinegar on Lye

RECENTLY, I HAD to tell my friends that I had suffered a severe disappointment. I had been pinning my hopes on something, and now those hopes had been dashed. I was sad, but I wasn't feeling particularly needy; my expectations of sympathy were not unduly high. But what surprised me was the consistency of the reaction. Almost everyone replied with instantaneous optimism: "Oh well, when one door shuts another is bound to open." Even friends who are not particularly devout quickly came up with a religious interpretation: "God obviously has something else in mind. Just you wait and see. This is obviously 'meant to be.'" And some who are usually quite original in the way they talk came out with clichés about "clouds that have silver linings"!

In the end I couldn't remember a single reply that was not in some form or another a changing of the subject. Under the guise of positive thinking and hope everyone had shifted the conversation away from my sadness. Of course, I had politely agreed to move on with them: "Yes, of course, when one door shuts another opens." But later I had to admit to myself that their optimism was a symptom of their unwillingness to stay for a moment with me in my grief, just as it was. It was a failure of companionship. If companionship means sharing bread, the only bread I had just then was, in the old words of the Bible, the bread of affliction. It had been politely refused even by those who love me.

My experience is, of course, as old as the hills. The book of Proverbs in the Bible has a rueful verse about the way we actually make things worse for those who suffer when we try to hastily cheer them up: "Like one who takes off a garment on a cold day, like vinegar on lye, is one who sings songs to a heavy heart" (25:20). Ministry and mutual care are full of these paradoxes. When we hastily prescribe a dose of "looking on the bright side" to our friends who are sad we can hurt them more than the original cause of their sadness. Answers that sound very spiritual and uplifting, when ill-timed, can do more harm than good.

And when the message of optimism is repeated, it can signal that feelings of sadness ought not to be expressed. Perhaps we should be ashamed of these feelings. Next time, we will be more cautious about expressing the negative things in our lives, and we will push negative feelings down inside. Yet there they can fester as untended wounds, and the infection of resentment can follow.

The New Testament ethic summed up as "Rejoice with those who rejoice, weep with those who weep" (Rom. 12:15) may seem simple, but it epitomizes an entire spirituality with demanding disciplines and skills that most of us have difficulty learning. In fact, a great deal of ministry requires the spirit that the Chinese know as *wu-wei,* which means "non-action." It is a matter of not acting out our desire to fix something or somebody. It means neither trying to control, nor giving in to, our discomfort at the proximity of suffering. Non-action accepts our urge to "change the subject" from the other's pain, but doesn't implement it. It involves humility, letting the sufferer be the one who knows when to move on, not ourselves. It is the sufferer's pain, and she has the right to hold the note of grieving in her song for as long as she needs.

Oddly enough, even those of us who tend to interfere with the suffering of others by quickly telling them what it means and how to cheer up or move on have experienced the paradox of consolation. We remember how it actually feels more encouraging when someone responds to our own pain with a very simple confirmation of our right to feel as sad as we do, whether it is a simple "That really sucks" or "I wish I could take that burden from you." And in the early stages of our grieving what we want is not to be alone. If a friend can't simply stay by our side for a while with us in impotence and sadness, but has to move on to the more optimistic ground where he is more comfortable, then he has risked making us feel abandoned as well as wounded.

The practice of *wu-wei* can give a true ability to be silent with those in pain. Grief doesn't need all this talking and fixing. Sometimes, we find friends who know how to stay quietly with us in our disappointments and let us make our own pace. When I went to work as a young volunteer in the first hospice where the modern hospice movement began, I was petrified that I wouldn't know what to say to the dying. I quickly learned that they really appreciate those who don't try to force everything into words, but will hold them very gently and stick around them willingly and quietly. I remember a young Scotsman dying of cancer who would not talk to anyone about dying, and I was lost for words around him. But as I gradually got used to just going about the routines of nursing I accepted that I didn't need to fix anything with words, not even his silence. He broke that silence when he was ready, and I felt privileged when he finally murmured to me, "I shall be glad when this is over."

8
Going Overboard

AS A CHILD, I couldn't figure out why so many other people couldn't detect all sorts of scents that I picked up. Eventually, I realized that the powerful sense of smell that both my grandmother and I were endowed with was quite exceptional. (The latest research has confirmed that the sense of smell in some people can be as much as eighty times stronger than the norm.) Perhaps this is why I naturally respond to the imagery of aroma in the scriptures, which is often overlooked. The Easter stories themselves are suffused with olfactory memories. Jesus was buried with a fantastically extravagant quantity of spices—a hundred pounds of myrrh and aloes—and even this hadn't seemed enough to the women who had prepared his body, and who were intent on returning after the Sabbath with yet more. I think of the beloved disciple crouching in the tomb to verify the stunning news that the body was missing, and then turning to look out at the rising sun. The perfume of the spices he was crunching underfoot must have been overpowering. The aroma would have been pouring out from the tomb into the dawn air.

The gospels tell us that there was something about Jesus that made people go completely overboard with perfume. The astrologers who tracked him down to Bethlehem in the first weeks of his life left him their entire supply of myrrh and incense, with gold to buy more when that ran out. The woman who was so desperate to demonstrate her gratitude to Jesus for his message of forgiveness gate-crashed Simon the Pharisee's private dinner party and poured a year's supply of imported perfume onto Jesus' feet. When Lazarus and Martha entertained Jesus to dinner before the final Passover they must have thought "It's déjà vu all over again" when Mary anointed Jesus with an entire jar full of Indian perfume. "The house was filled with the fragrance of the perfume." But it made Judas Iscariot sick to his stomach with resentment. He just couldn't hold back from trying to cancel out the exaltation and beauty of her gesture with moralism: "Why was this perfume not sold and the money given to the poor?" (John 12:3–6; Mark 14:3–9).

In answering Judas, Jesus made a promise: "Truly I tell you, wherever the good news is proclaimed in the whole world, what she has done will be told in remembrance of her." The promise has come true. The pouring out of perfume in a gesture of reckless love has itself become part of the good news as an image of what has happened through the life and death and resurrection of Jesus. God has released into the world the only thing that can ultimately win us. Even God cannot win us by coercion. We can only be won by attraction, by love. The myrrh and the aloes of the Easter tomb, the ointment of nard poured over Jesus, the frankincense left at his cradle—all these are specifically mentioned in the Song of Songs, the book of scripture that most revels in the erotic splendors of scent and which was read as an allegory of the ultimate love affair, the Creator's ardent courtship of the human race and of each and every human being.

I suspect that the apostle Paul had a good nose, appreciative of the incense used in outdoor processions and of the perfumes sold in the bazaars. Perhaps like me in airport duty-free shops, he couldn't always resist the free samples of colognes at the perfumers' stalls. In his second letter to the

Corinthians, he gets us to imagine ourselves as God's incredibly attractive aroma.

> But thanks be to God, who in Christ always leads us in triumphal procession, and through us spreads in every place the fragrance that comes from knowing him. For we are the aroma of Christ to God among those who are being saved and among those who are perishing; to the one a fragrance from death to death, to the other a fragrance from life to life. (2 Cor. 2:14–16)

It is an extraordinary image for everyday evangelism. Evangelism is spreading "in every place the fragrance that comes from knowing him." We are the "aroma of Christ." The power of the risen Christ is the power to attract, and by knowing him ourselves, by following our attraction, we acquire and transmit his allure. As members of his body, we exert his attractiveness in the world. We don't hear this imagery preached very often. Passionate it is, but not sentimental. Paul knows full well that many people think the gospel of a crucified Messiah stinks as a message—and by association we will stink as well. In holding their noses at the gospel and at us, they will become even more set in their ways. To those we are "a fragrance from death to death."

These disturbing metaphors can help us to refocus our expectations about how discipleship actually works out in real life. Our calling is to express in our everyday behavior the attractiveness of a compassionate God. If we do, we will play a part in drawing some people to a new life in Christ. And yet if we are being true to the Christ who was crucified, we will also provoke incomprehension, condescension, and outright anger in others.

9
"O–My–God!"

CHANNEL SURFING IS a vice, but the bizarre collages that it flashes before our gaze are sometimes curiously effective in revealing the obsessions that grip our culture. Men blasting away at each other with guns in the action thrillers; the cosmetic surgeons relentlessly plying their scalpels and suction tubes in the extreme makeover programs—and then there are the constantly recurring "ta-daa!" scenes in which complacent decorators invite householders back into their homes to see the miraculous results of the makeover efforts. The scenes are absolutely predictable. Hands fly up to the face in amazement and the cry goes up, "O—my—God!" Exactly the same happens in the fashion shows that work wondrous transformations on the plain and unfashionable. "O—my—God!" the friends exclaim in rapture when the women or men reemerge from behind the scenes and smile winsomely in their unaccustomed glamour.

These exclamations of the divine name of God are now automatic. Perhaps they indicate that these new kinds of consumerist ritual really are stealing the primal theme of transfiguration from religion and taking it over for the idolatrous purpose of worshiping the surface glamour conferred by cosmetics and clothes. Now we are adding this profanation of the name of God to the other conventional forms already embedded in everyday speech. The name of God is the second most common expletive to use when we hit our thumb with a hammer. People use it to intensify bitter scolding: "My *God,* you are so clumsy!...*Jesus!* When will you ever learn?" It is completely unthinking and all-pervasive.

I was dealing with a problem at work the other day and my colleague was getting so exasperated with his own problem that he shouted out, "Jesus H. Christ!" while smacking the desk with his fist. And something clicked inside. I overheard myself saying calmly, "You know, since I worship Jesus Christ, it's really painful to hear you use his name like that." My soul must have been insisting that it isn't healthy to inure myself to the abuse of the name of Christ, to just let it go—although that is easier. Who wants to risk seeming "holier than thou"? As it happens, the one I was talking to is of another faith. And far from resenting my response, he took it seriously as an entirely appropriate reaction from someone who actually does revere Jesus. He sincerely apologized. (In my heart, I also asked for God's forgiveness, because I was acutely aware, even as I spoke, of my own usual complicity in the vulgar habit of using Jesus' name as a virtual swearword or an inane exclamation of amazement.)

We repeatedly pray in the Lord's Prayer, "Hallowed be your name," and yet hardly any of us seem to know what that means. It is as if the very meaning of the word "hallow" now eludes us. It must mean much more than merely refraining from abusing God's name as an expletive, though that is a first step. In this urgent and prophetic prayer Jesus is calling on God to sanctify his name at long last, to restore its holiness and fullness of meaning after we have demeaned it and soiled it. Surely his inspiration was the awesome thirty-sixth chapter of the prophecy of Ezekiel, in which the seer expresses the conviction that God will take action to restore his own reputation, which his own people have degraded by their faithlessness:

> I will sanctify my great name, which has been pro-
> faned among the nations, and which you have pro-
> faned among them; and the nations shall know that I
> am the LORD, says the Lord GOD, when *through you* I
> display my holiness before their eyes. (Ezek. 36:23)

The prophet makes clear that God can only restore the glory of his defiled and abused name through us, by changing us, by manifesting holiness in our lives. So the prophecy continues by emphasizing that the only way God can re-sanctify his name that we have allowed to become soiled and empty is by transforming us from the inside out:

> A new heart I will give you, and a new spirit I will
> put within you; and I will remove from your body the
> heart of stone and give you a heart of flesh. (36:26)

The prophet says that God will have hallowed his name when we have hearts of flesh again. He doesn't say we need a heart of gold. God re-glorifies his name as he restores our lost humanity back to us. He wants us to be human, to have hearts of flesh. The coming of Jesus is not to make us super-human, but to heal our inhumanity, to turn the stoniness of our hearts into responsiveness, vulnerability, imagination, and creativity. When we learn to pray "Hallowed be your name!" we are opening ourselves to that very transformation.

In the silly television shows the participants squeal "O—my—God!" in response to surface glitz. But to hallow God's name is to appeal from the heart to the One hidden within it, reserving the exclamation "O my God!" for the expression of our love for the only one who can make our hearts over from within.

10
Basenji Worship

FRIENDS WHO ARE familiar with my ways will sometimes blurt out "Uh oh!" when we are walking along a street, a signal they have caught sight of something that is bound to cause a delay. A Basenji has come into view, and they know there will have to be a pause for Basenji worship. Basenjis are an ancient breed of dog, originating in the Congo. They look slightly like a robust version of a small deer, usually russet in color with white markings and a tail that curls back like a spring. They have all sorts of exotic features, wash themselves as fastidiously as cats, and yodel rather than bark. Their brows are usually wrinkled in an expression of perpetual curiosity and concern, and their ears are always pricked up in alertness. And they can jump vertically into the air.

I will cross the street and drop to one knee in front of the handsome dog, if the owner will indulge me, and make the kind of reverential fuss that we who love the breed must perform. Careful not to exhaust the patience of my friends, the owner, or the dog (Basenjis don't lose their dignity), I know to move on after a moment, elated from the chance to pay homage.

The word "worship" may sound like a facetious exaggeration, but it can be defended as a testimony to the sacredness of the bond that we can have with animals. The source of my devotion is simple enough to explain. The dog I most loved as a child was a Basenji—a friend who was moving left her in our care—and the mere sight of one will fill me with brimming emotions of tenderness and gratitude for all the pleasure she gave me. And these blissful sensations are sacred at depth, because we can hardly be prepared for a blissful relationship with God if we don't have experiences that open our hearts to bliss, and forge the neural circuits in our brains and bodies that enable us to register profound delight. And if we are honest, we might admit that certain animals in their own unique ways have been as effective in communicating certain aspects of God's love to us as other human beings have been. The grief we experience when they die can be as searing as our mourning for human loved ones.

I suppose there is a danger in thinking that it is only our relationships with pet animals that are sacred, because we tend to humanize them, pretending that they are more like us than they really are. But true sacredness always impresses us with a sense of *otherness*, and we can't recognize the sacred character of our relationships with the animal world until we honor their radical otherness. Human beings are only one species, and we belong in an immense continuum with others who vastly outnumber us and differ from us in staggeringly varied ways. True wisdom honors the mysterious otherness of the animal world as God-given. I have always been deeply impressed with the centrality of this theme in one of the least understood books of the Bible, the book of Job. This extraordinary part of scripture insists on the contemplation of the animal kingdom in its startling non-human otherness as a critical necessity for human self-understanding before God.

The book of Job explores the problem of innocent suffering through the story of a good man whose faithfulness is tested by catastrophe. God allows his prosecuting attorney, the Satan, to inflict illness and ruin on Job to test his reactions. Job responds by challenging God and arguing with his friends in an exhaustive debate that goes on for thirty-seven chapters. His friends are sure that Job must have done something to deserve punishment, but Job insists he is innocent and accuses God of being arbitrary and unjust in letting him suffer. Finally, God ends the discussion by confronting Job in person.

God's response is awe-inspiring and very strange. He doesn't resolve the enigma of human suffering with some kind of philosophical theory. Instead, to our bafflement, God replies with a long interrogation that tests Job's knowledge about nature, specifically the bizarre behavior patterns of such creatures as the ostrich, the hippopotamus, and the crocodile. They defy human logic:

> The ostrich's wings flap wildly,
>   though its pinions lack plumage.
> For it leaves its eggs to the earth,
>   and lets them be warmed on the ground,
> forgetting that a foot may crush them,
>   and that a wild animal may trample them.
> It deals cruelly with its young, as if they were
>   not its own;
>   though its labor should be in vain, yet it has
>   no fear;
> because God has made it forget wisdom,
>   and given it no share in understanding. (39:13–17)

God's stern test of Job's scientific observation of the natural world is specifically designed to emphasize that God did not create the world using a human template. The animal world in all its glorious otherness is a magnificent warning against the pretensions of the human imagination to make sense of the world, including the prevalence of pain, on exclusively human terms.

The message is as relevant today as it was twenty-five centuries ago. Most religious ideas of God as a being who manipulates events to punish or reward us are fictions. True wisdom accepts the complexity and strangeness of life itself and knows that life does not conform to simplistic human theories of cause and effect. God humbles us humans to recognize ourselves as creatures within a much larger ecological continuum that includes all the animals. Instead of fabricating clumsy theories about merit and punishment, we do better to accept our vulnerability as part of the risks of life, and devote our energies to wonder and gratitude instead of resentment and defensiveness. Only after God gives Job a long and intricate lecture about crocodile behavior does Job recognize the futility of his complaints and repent. His change of mind consists of being reinstated by God's tough-love ecological lecture into the mysterious, complex, interrelated world of creatureliness.

11
New Sacred Stories

IT ISN'T OFTEN that a television program literally brings me to my knees, but I found myself needing to hunker down to pray after the final program in a series that has been presenting new knowledge about the evolution of our species, and striking theories about the routes by which our pioneering ancestors migrated from Africa to populate the planet, based on genetic testing of population samples from all over the globe. It is hard to imagine a question closer to the heart of religion than "Where did we human beings come from? How did we get here?"

One fascinating scene stood out as a telling pointer to one of the most critical spiritual dilemmas of the beginning of the twenty-first century. The researcher was telling a group of Navajo elders about discoveries he had made using new techniques for tracing genetic markers in DNA. They demonstrated that Navajo ancestry can be traced to a tribe whose current members are still nomadic reindeer herders in the extreme northeast of Siberia. It was impossible not to be moved by the dilemma his listeners faced. Navajo religious creation legends tell a quite different story: far from being migrants, the original ancestors were born from the womb of the very land they now occupy. Keeping this ancestral myth alive is considered crucial to preserving Navajo cultural identity. The elders were impressed with the new scientific ideas and a map that could trace the thread of human migration out of Africa, through Siberia, down to the American continent. But you could see how vulnerable they felt in the face of "authoritative" western science, which threatens to overwhelm and displace their stories and those of all other indigenous peoples.

Looming in the background of this conversation was yet another account of human origins, to which the presenter and the tribal elders never alluded, the story that has dominated the western world for centuries. This is, of course, the biblical story of human origins, the story of a universe created in seven days six thousand years ago: a single original human couple, Adam and Eve, whose descendants were annihilated in a catastrophic world flood, save for a few who escaped in Noah's ark and became the ancestors of all human beings.

As I knelt to pray after the program, I just needed to stay with the confusion that comes from trying to hold together disparate creation stories. It is a confusion that many of us are struggling with. We hear one story in church read in scripture, underlying the prayers and hymns, and depicted in sacred art. Out of that church context, we watch with fascination as a common narrative of human origins forged by entirely new scientific tools emerges for the very first time in human history, a big picture integrated into new knowledge of the history of our planet and its myriad species. And we are also aware of the creation myths of countless tribes and peoples all over the world, and how they are threatened with extinction.

Fundamentalists who are insistently presenting a literal version of the biblical story of creation as strictly historical and uniquely scientific and denouncing secular accounts of evolution as godless propaganda, though misguided, at least sense the magnitude of the crisis. Religion can't thrive long if we divide ourselves into watertight compartments, repeating in church the sacred stories of Adam and Eve and the flood and then hearing an entirely different story in our schools and on a Nova broadcast. Avoiding the quest for a unified vision of Creator and creation by switching back and forth between "sacred" and "secular" accounts isn't the answer.

Now it may be early days for this new emerging common scientific narrative of human origins, but the task of integrating it spiritually can't be put off. *Our challenge is to explore this new story as intrinsically sacred.* If the Spirit leads us into all truth, the Spirit is stirring us to release the divine splendor latent in it, through prayer and praise. A thrilling scientific story of the evolution and migration of our species is now being articulated with unprecedented dramatic detail. If it is true, then God's creative presence throughout it, God's companioning of emergent humanity in it, can and must be articulated in theology and hymn and prayer.

When we proclaim that humankind was made in the image and likeness of God, can we integrate into that conviction our new awareness that numerous humanoid species have walked this planet before us, and that we are the sole survivors? Human beings have a special and unique relationship with the Creator of the universe. Can we imagine a God who was also in some unfathomable and poignant way the God of the Neanderthals, who faded away with the arrival of modern humans in their territory? Can we include in our sacred creation story the sudden annihilation of the dinosaurs in a global catastrophe that opened up the evolutionary opportunity for mammals—such as ourselves—to evolve? Can we write hymns and liturgies that let us sing our hearts out about the awesome mysteries of evolution? Can we both honor the revelatory power of our biblical creation myths, and also turn new science into prayer and praise?

I believe that it was God bringing me to my knees after watching the television program, and it is God who will incite us to achieve this new spiritual integration.

Compass

12
No Choice but to Choose

WHENEVER I VISIT my family in New Zealand I make a pilgrimage to the South Island to explore glaciers. *Pilgrimage* is the right word because it is a profound spiritual experience to stand above the rain forest and contemplate the majestic forces that shaped so much of the landscapes we inhabit. Maybe that is why I am impressed with an image that the renowned historian of mythology Joseph Campbell used to illuminate the religious landscape we live in now at the beginning of the twenty-first century. He talks about living at the "terminal moraine" of mythology. A terminal moraine is the mass of mixed rock and debris that the glacier collects over its slow progress and then dumps at the end of its journey where the ice finally melts. These massive heaps contain very diverse materials from many places.

This image of the terminal moraine helps us to recognize our unique situation in humankind's spiritual journey. For thousands of years our ancestors created a vast array of myths and rituals and legends about the presence and action of divinity in the world. The spiritual history of humankind has been like a huge glacier detaching myths and legends from their original context and adding them to the rest as it grinds relentlessly on. And now the process of religious mythmaking has come to a standstill. Science now rules as the primary tool for making meaning. We who are believers and trust that there has been genuine revelation to our ancestors live at the terminal moraine that has all their traditions and beliefs dumped in front of us. We are the first generation in history that has access to almost all the religious traditions of our predecessors at once. Even stories from the obscurest tribes can be Googled! What are we to make of all these deposits of tradition? Well, we can't make much of them *all*—we have to select from them. We have to choose which traditions have life in them for today, and which beliefs, legends, and teachings are obsolete; what we can use and own, and what we must leave behind.

This *having to choose* is what makes being an aware believer today both stressful and exciting. For most of human history, believers didn't have to choose. Traditional religions insisted that the ancestors and the spiritual forces they encountered had done all the choosing for us in the ancient times. It was for us to pass on the traditions through ritual. It is scary to shoulder the burden of responsibility now of discerning that some religious traditions are worth conserving and some need to be jettisoned. It isn't hard to understand the anxiety that fuels so much traditionalism. Traditionalists try to insist that we don't really have to choose. There is an already existing package deal called orthodoxy. Our role is to take it as a whole or leave it. (Traditionalists have usually avoided facing the actual reality that all orthodoxies were formed through drawn-out processes of selection.)

The anxieties of traditionalists are often projected against "the liberals" precisely for daring to "pick and choose" from the tradition; scathing remarks about "cafeteria religion" are typical. It is possible to empathize with their hostility. There is something worrisome about the attitude that we are now free to assemble our religious beliefs and practices from a bit here and a bit there, according to our individual desires. The deepest spiritual traditions are those that reveal that our individual leanings are warped by evasion and bias. And they are rarely as personal as we think. Our blind spots and preferences are often simply the ways we have succumbed to the collective prejudices and illusions of our own cultures. So conservatives interpret the ordination of women, for example, or a positive regard for same-sex couples, as instances where authentic traditions have been sacrificed under the pressure to conform to contemporary mores.

It is a very deep issue in contemporary spirituality: How do we learn to pray about this responsibility of making choices? To put it crudely, traditionalists seem to suggest a God who will *abandon us* if we pick and choose. Liberals seem to suggest a God who has *left us on our own* to pick and choose. But in fact we won't be abandoned and we haven't been left. Rather, God embraces us and struggles with us in the process of choosing. The real issue of choosing what to believe is learning to recognize who God yearns to be for us now. It is a matter of God's yearning to be known now. And we can be perfectly certain from the very nature of the gospel that God yearns to relieve us of the burden of images and ideas that do not express who God wants to be for us now.

God knows—and this is no mere expression—God knows it isn't easy to discern what has gone dead among religious traditions and what is still alive, flowing with the current of divine energy and liberating love. Because God knows, prayer is the key to the responsible act of discerning what to lay aside and what to make our own from the tradition. There is no substitute for conversation that comes clean about the struggle to know what to believe, a conversation that shouldn't be just with ourselves in the form of worry, but a conversation with a God who is keeping us company. "God, who do you want to be for me? How do you want us to know you today?"

13
Put Out That Fire

RECENTLY A FRIEND wandered into a lunchtime
service at a thriving Anglican church in London. In his
address, the minister mentioned that he had recently been to
the Cathedral of Saint John the Divine in New York and had
seen a notice about a forthcoming visit by the Dalai Lama.
Well, no doubt the Dalai Lama was a "nice enough person"
but unless he accepted Jesus Christ as his personal savior, he
would "perish." My friend noticed the speaker's half-smile at
this point, a smile mirrored by approving glances among the
congregation. Knowing smiles of complicity—"perish" was
a code word to mean "tortured forever in hell." Nice people have ways of getting round the crude assertion of hell. A
movie star who is an ultraconservative Roman Catholic said
in a recent interview that he believed his (Protestant) wife
might not "make it" in the afterlife. He figured he didn't
have to spell out what "not making it" meant in his belief
system.

Perhaps working for the Holocaust Museum has scraped
my skin thinner, but I can't bear the politeness of religious
sadism, these smiles about hell. They remind me of the
euphemisms like "final solution" that the Nazi officials who
tortured millions to death used to cover their work of creating hell on earth. It appears that some of these sadists had
spiritual resources to help them cope with the demands of

their work. You can find Adolf Eichman's signature in the guest book of a monastery overlooking the Danube where he went on retreat as a young SS officer. The technocrat of massacre might need meditation to keep going.

What is horrifying is that so many religious people can contemplate the eternal torments of billions with such calmness. The Nazi killing machines ran for a few terrible years. But torture that can never end as *God's eternal work*. . .! And it is a calmness that sometimes verges on relish. Perhaps the half-smile that played on the lips of the clergyman talking about the doom awaiting the Dalai Lama betrays the psychological dynamic behind the speculation discussed by medieval theologians who proposed that awareness of the sufferings of the damned in hell actually enhances the joy of the saints in heaven. This is sadism, voyeuristic pleasure in violence.

Many of those who reject traditional Christianity do so on moral grounds. They sincerely feel themselves, flawed as they are, to be more compassionate, more humane, less violent, less sadistic, than a God who, so it is said, intends to sustain billions of creatures in existence so they can be tortured forever. They cannot allow themselves to believe in a God supposedly capable of such limitless violence.

Traditional teaching about eternal damnation in Christianity and Islam excites further disgust by its link with the religiously motivated violence that is all too real and pervasive in the world around us. Confidence that God is going to torture one's opponents for all eternity fuels the cycle of retaliatory political violence. The suicide bomber can discount the momentary suffering of those he is blowing up, because it is nothing compared with the torments of the eternal hell to which his God is going to condemn them. The God-who-sends-to-hell can be invoked to sanction each successive round of retaliation. Crusade, jihad, anti-Semitism, religiously sanctioned violence: all these horrors are now playing out before our gaze on the nightly news.

Openhearted Christians will have to be braver in resolving the internal contradictions within our own religion, which has passed on to us this fearful mythology of eternal torture mixed up with another message of love based on what Paul called the foolishness and weakness of the message of the cross. The Word that makes present a wholly nonviolent and vulnerable God of compassion and forgiveness, who sanctions and inspires only love, reconciliation, forgiveness, tenderness, healing, and community, seems laughably powerless. But if the foolishness of God is going to get a hearing through our lips we must embrace it more passionately. Those who preach the God who sends to hell have a terrific advantage—the traditional language has a lot of red-blooded potency. In contrast, language about Jesus' radical nonviolence and the message of the cross often sounds colorless and anemic. We need to kiss the sleeping language of nonviolence awake in church.

We talk of embracing the way of nonviolence, and a wholly nonviolent God needs our very warmest embrace. We have to bring our erotic energy, our passion, our vital capacity for love in every sense to meet the God of desire and tenderness revealed in the gospel. We need language to evoke the presence of such a God and invite others to such a path, an erotic religious language that dances and sings to woo and wow us.

What can you do to speak of the vulnerability of God, the passion and tenderness of God, the hot, warm, electric power of compassion, the delight of peace, the beauty of self-giving and forgiveness, the virile and fertile power of nonviolent action? The stream flowing from the side of Christ crucified flowed to put out the fires of hell. Let's get flowing. This is what Holy Spirit is.

14
Fault Lines

"LEAD US NOT into temptation" is probably the least understood petition in the Lord's Prayer, and one we usually repeat merely by rote. The word *peirasmos* doesn't mean what we usually think of as temptation, being lured to committing a misdeed. It refers to the final great ordeal that was expected before the coming of God's reign, an ordeal so severe that even the faithful few might cave in and desert God's cause. The prayer is to be spared the kind of test that might break our spirit. To make the prayer our own today requires us to meditate on the kind of stresses that really put our loyalty to God to the test. It presupposes that we have taken the measure of flaws in our character which would give way under pressure. And we need to make this prayer a truly corporate prayer, not just an individual one, so that we can pray about the "fault lines" in the church where it can disintegrate under stress.

As people talk to me about the current conflicts in the church around homosexuality and issues of authority many of them show that they are aware that they present a major spiritual test. Many intuitively sense that the danger doesn't lie in the controversial issues themselves—whether some churches are committing apostasy by blessing gay unions or others are misunderstanding the way that the Bible is authoritative. The real danger lies in the way controversy itself can become corrosive. Terrible damage is done to our souls when we fling anathemas at one another and get satisfaction from despising those with whom we disagree. Controversy is one of those trials in which we are truly vulnerable, and our spirituality is not worth much if it fails to give us tools for protecting ourselves against being wounded and poisoned, and from harming others.

The theme of spiritual combat—inner struggle against the powers of evil—is not an easy one to make our own these days. The Bible speaks of the "whole armor of God" that helps us "quench all the flaming arrows of the evil one" (Eph. 6:11–16), but the imagery of armor and hand-to-hand combat with devils seems as remote and unreal as those stained glass windows of Arthurian knights in shining armor that were popular at the beginning of the last century. An alternative to imagery of hand-to-hand swordplay is offered in the Buddhist tradition, which speaks of "skillful means"—tried and tested methods of eluding and disarming the forces that can hook us into futile, destructive patterns of thinking and behaving.

Intercession is one of those skillful means, but if we pray for our "enemies"—those with opposing views in controversy—from a distance, asking God to enlighten and convert them, we can actually make things worse, intensifying our separateness. We need to find forms of intercession that dissolve the interior schism between us. One way—it is simple but not easy—is to imagine them kneeling with us, side by side, and ask God to enfold us together in a single embrace of love.

Another is the constant practice of letting go and handing over to God. Evil doesn't have to seduce most of us in dramatic ways. It is enough to trap us in preoccupation. Church conflicts can have that destructive power not because the antagonists and bystanders are bad people but because strife breeds fretting and fretting sucks the energy away from our creativity. We need to encourage one another with words like "I don't want to go over this again. I feel the need to refocus on something different. I need to let this go just now. . . ." Interiorly, it means practicing the most common form of putting one's trust in God, handing these complex matters over to God's hands, surrendering the burdensome anxiety that Jesus named as the very bane of our lives. God is like the patient master trying to get the dog to drop the bone on which it has clenched its jaws, urging us to "drop it." We can't take in the nourishment we need if our jaws are locked on a worry. Indeed, the word *worry* itself comes from the Anglo-Saxon word for an animal shaking the prey it has in its teeth.

Another important skill can be learned from a therapist or a wise spiritual director, who can catch us out when we are getting all worked up about some issue in our lives as a way of avoiding the deeper questions. They know not to get caught up in the drama and with some gentle questions can lead us back to the deeper questions, the ones that are much more creative. "You are focusing a lot on how your supervisor behaves at the office. How are things at home between you and your husband?"

Current controversies about sexuality throw a lot of light on what it means to negotiate testing situations that put our well-being in danger. Vehemently denouncing or defending the sex lives of others is great way to avoid facing the light and the shadow in our own intimate relationships. If we pray sincerely to God, "Lead us not into the time of trial," we would do well to spell that out by offering ourselves as healers in the church's struggles to deal with sexuality, rather than being angry partisans for one position or another. There is a deep spiritual dimension to sex that it takes courage to explore where there is so much polarization and obsession with the morality of gay sex. We need inspiration from those mystics who look deeper into the erotic dimension of life for rich intimations about God's desire for union with us. It is very tempting to focus on sexuality as a problem, especially a problem created by others, and we can survive the trial only if we are ready to face the deeper challenge of exploring our own experience of the erotic and asking questions about how the presence of the living God can be found in the human drive to find intimacy and bliss.

15

Clock-Watching

LAST WEEKEND OVER drinks, some friends and I were exchanging stories on the theme of our most memorable nights at the theater. I was happy to reminisce about an unforgettable performance by the Dance Theatre of Harlem I witnessed one winter's night in New York, twenty-five years ago. Several of us had alluded to the way great art can completely change our sense of time. It releases us from clock time into another dimension. The ballet was so vivifying that the audience seemed to lose track of time, and when the performance ended, instead of dispersing, hundreds of us lingered afterward in the snowy streets outside. Some bought boxes of chocolates from a store opposite and handed them around as a kind of spontaneous sacrament of the communion the performance had created among us.

These moments of altered consciousness make us aware of the tyranny of clock time in our western culture. We are conditioned to believe that only clock time is real and to accept as normative the harried clock-watching state we are trapped in. Those rare moments when time seems to slow down or stand still to allow us to tap deeper levels of experience and feeling assume an ever greater importance the more driven our schedules become.

It seems almost too much to ask for, and yet I dream of a church equipped to help us resist the tyranny of clock time. Such a church would make room for forms of worship designed to take away the pressure of watching the clock, worship that encourages us to enter a different level of awareness and receptivity, worship that opens us to a sense of eternity. It is a lot to ask for, because our current regular forms of worship are bound by rigid schedules. In many parishes virtually every service must be squeezed within one hour because we all need to be going on to the next thing. And the pace of many of our liturgies is quick-fire, as if we had to keep it going in order to get it over with in time. There's no room for spontaneity. And even though the rubrics specify certain pauses for silence during the Eucharist, actual attempts by the leaders of worship to observe them can be met with vigorous resistance from those in the congregation who regard silence as literally a waste of their time, rather than a chance to quietly commune.

Probably it isn't realistic to expect radical change in the pattern of our regular Sunday mornings, but that isn't the end of the story. The secret may lie in creating for ourselves occasional opportunities to worship in a different mode, where the rigid constraints of time are lifted and eternity has a better chance of breaking through our defenses.

Some of these opportunities can be very simple indeed. I have particularly cherished contemplative Eucharists which follow these very simple guidelines: a quiet, carpeted space cleared of furniture; worshipers hunkering down on the floor, kneeling or sitting on stools and cushions; no shoes, no watches, no books or service leaflets; a simple low table for the altar, a few candles, maybe a little incense. The worshipers learn a few simple chants beforehand in preparation, and the service unfolds in a leisurely way, allowing lengthy breathing spaces. We actually have time to let the readings sink in. The homily comes out of silence and then returns to it. There's no hurry to cease a particular chant as long as it is lifting up our hearts. There's ample time to examine our hearts before confession, to prepare in adoration to receive communion, to linger in thankful appreciation after receiving. And the celebrant can improvise the eucharistic prayer in a rare, lovely experience of not being stuck in the book. Time again I have heard people say that during these Eucharists they lost track of time; they had no idea that they had it in them to just let go and *be* in the present moment with God. Maybe we spent an hour and a half, and yet it might seem longer to some and shorter to others.

At the opposite end of the spectrum is the experience of festal liturgies and liturgies of pilgrimage where people gather in greater numbers than most of our average Sunday congregations. If the full potential of these occasions can be realized, especially through the grandeur of heartfelt singing and chanting en masse, and the practice of rituals that help us use both sides of our brains, they can be times when we experience the transcending of individuality through the Spirit and a powerful sense of integration as the body of Christ. And once again, a symptom of our collective entry into that different state of consciousness will be a sense of liberation from clock time. Sometime it takes travel to be reminded of the power of this kind of worship, whether it is in African worship, with its freedom to devote hours to allowing this experience of transcendence to emerge, or in the liturgies of the Orthodox churches, whose rhythms deliberately unwind us from our tense subordination to the clock.

My friends and I had no trouble sharing experiences of "timelessness" in the theater. How many of us would have stories of parallel experiences in church? We should talk to one another about this and see. Surely, if the church were what it claims to be, it would be even better at providing glimpses of eternity than the stage.

16
Entrance Ticket

"I HAVE SOME problems with the creed," I overheard someone say after church recently, and it struck me that the admission was very like those we make about close relationships: "I'm having problems with my eldest son. . . ." Can we have a relationship with the creeds? Can we love them? Can we have an understanding with them? As I thought about it, I realized that I *did* have feelings for the creeds, feelings associated with four images: an entrance ticket, a coin, the list of contents in a book of poems, and a song.

First, *an entrance ticket*. In the early church the creeds were called the "symbols." At baptism, the new convert would recite the "symbol" of faith. To me there is the encouraging suggestion that the creed is a constellation of metaphors and images all crying out for interpretation. All talk about God is through symbols. But there is more to this title "symbol." Northrop Frye, one of the greatest literary interpreters of the Bible, reminds us that "originally a symbol was a token or counter, like the stub of a theater ticket which is not the performance but will take us to where the performance is." The creeds were originally created to summarize for converts what baptism was going to let them into. Reciting the baptismal symbol, they were admitted to the drama. The priest was like a theater usher welcoming them into the arena of Christian worship, prayer, and practice. Once inside, they would experience for themselves what it means to worship the Creator, to have a relationship with Christ, to experience forgiveness, to have resurrection hope.

A coin. Coins have to be made of alloy to work. Coins made of pure metals are too soft; constant handling quickly rubs off the image and inscription. In the same way creeds are not meant to be the "pure gold" of inspired spiritual teaching. The creeds are not the perfect summary of Christian faith. They were assembled in some awkward ways in the early councils. They might sound clunky, and not express the essentials in the way we might choose today. But they were created as common coin for use, and their value has held up over sixteen centuries of very rough handling. They deserve honor for holding together a common identity for Christians separated by culture and distance, and for being the legacy that generation has handed to generation. If we could get more emotional about the creed, it might move us to tears to think of the millions who have recited them before us, and who do so today—some of them with their dying breath as martyrs.

A list of contents in a book of poems. A friend once handed me a little book of poetry, Elizabeth Barrett Browning's *Sonnets from the Portuguese.* After reading a page, I commented, "The language is lovely, but I can't quite grasp what she is trying to say in this sonnet." The friend snatched the book back and exclaimed at once, "You didn't read one of the sonnets. You read the list of contents—all the first lines!" Embarrassing, but a pointer to what the creeds really are. They are lists of first lines, chapter headings. They have little meaning in and of themselves. It means virtually nothing to say, "He ascended into heaven." That is just the agenda item of a deep discussion about who Christ is, how Christ in present in the world today, how Christ's sovereignty is expressed. The creeds point us to the activity of exploring the meaning of our faith in community. We can't expect the chapter headings of the creed to have much meaning for us if we won't join in the exploration and discussion. Symbols cry out for interpretation.

Finally, *a song.* I'm used to singing the creeds in church and I'm always disappointed in services where they are said. This flat, monotonous recitation doesn't help us get emotionally connected, as singing does. The creeds are not official confessions of faith or catechisms as much as songs of defiance and the jubilant celebrations of tremendous mysteries. This was brought home to me as a young priest during my travels in the Soviet Union at a time when the communist regime banned all religious activities except the liturgy. I remember worshiping in a church in Kiev filled with the poor, mainly elderly *babushkas* and their grandchildren. When the moment came for the people to join the choir in singing the creed, suddenly a tremor of energy passed through the church. The fervor of the people's singing made the creed sound like the repeated crashing of the waves of an invincible sea. Tears streamed down my face, and I was not alone. And in fact their faith was an invincible tide. Twenty years later all the vast intellectual apparatus of Marxist-Leninist ideology collapsed into rubble almost overnight. The praise song of the creed is ridiculed as antiquated rubbish by the powerful—but this vast shout of praise and defiance goes on.

17
Dirty Work

MINISTRY. MINISTRIES. Overused church words that sometimes feel paper-thin, trodden completely flat by repetition. Words that urgently need rescuing from banality. A celebrated sermon by Sir Edwyn Hoskyns, one of the last century's great Anglican biblical scholars, spoke of the spiritual task of reviving exhausted words: "Can we rescue a word and discover a universe? Can we study a language and awake to the truth? Can we bury ourselves in a lexicon and arise in the presence of God...?" When we do go to the lexicon and trace the original metaphors that lie at the root of words, we often discover vivid and surprising images beneath the surface of terms we take for granted.

I recently celebrated the thirty-fifth anniversary of my ordination to the diaconate, so I have been thinking about *diakonia,* the Greek word we commonly translate as ministry. It derives from the words *dia,* through, and *konis,* meaning dust or grit. The original image behind Christian service and ministry is activity that takes you through the dust. The great Anglican bishop and divine Lancelot Andrewes always insisted that every kind of office in the church is a form of deaconing, "on foot and through the dust, for so is the nature of the word." Ministry refers to something close to the ground, a continuous journey through the grit and grime of the everyday. The word contradicts everything grandiose, lofty, or even sublime. Ministry is quite literally dirty work. Ministry always deals with the nitty-gritty of real human needs and struggles.

If the Greek word emphasizes the "gritty" aspect of ministry, the Latin emphasizes the "nitty." I remember being surprised when I first learned that our word "ministry" comes from the Latin root for small things, as in the word *miniscule*. It had never occurred to me, even though I am trained in the classical languages. Of course! A minister is a person involved in little matters, small affairs. A magister is responsible for big affairs and large issues.

If we took to heart the lesson of the lexicon, that ministry is linked with small things, we might be less subject to self-doubt. Few of us, lay or ordained, have big lives, with careers that make a huge visible impact in the public sphere. Our lives and our ministries seem to deal with such ordinary things that it is often difficult to grasp their lasting impact. The ways we touch each other's lives are often fleeting and unnoticed. The visit to the hospital, the offer of encouragement, the session in the after-school tutoring program, the sermon, the Sunday school class, the hour of counseling: the scale of such activities can seem so small. Do they make much difference?

It is healthier to pray about the doubt that hovers around all ministry than to brush it aside. At some level all of us want to make a difference, to leave a legacy, to change for the better the world we are passing through. If we have a gnawing sense that not much that we do really makes a difference, it can sap our motivation. It can tempt us to rationalize apathy and inaction. The call to ministry is one that demands that we confront our tendency to go along with the belief that little acts, small gestures, and everyday service don't count.

The entire thrust of the gospel, of course, is based on the contrast between the apparent value of those whose actions are public and dramatically effective and the apparent worthlessness of the unnoticed actions of the "little ones." We speak often of "empowerment" these days, and we run the risk of deluding ourselves that this means gaining access to the same kind of control enjoyed by the powerful. Christ empowered ordinary people by unlocking the secret that hidden and small actions have enormous transformative potential when we understand them as expressions of God's energies. Our small gestures and everyday acts of service are in fact our active participation in that encompassing web and force-field of love and hope known as the reign of God or the communion of the Holy Spirit.

The long conversations at the Last Supper that we find in John's gospel are a rich resource for meditation on the value God puts on the little gestures and actions that mainly comprise our ministries. In these final teachings of Jesus, John has him returning again and again to themes of ministry. Jesus speaks with astonishing humility about the fact—and it is a fact!—that those who choose to follow his way of service would achieve far more than he could in his short ministry: "Very truly, I tell you, the one who believes in me will also do the works that I do and, in fact, will do greater works than these, because I am going to the Father" (14:12). And he speaks about the lasting reality of works of ministry, their eternal worth as gifts that are actually building up God's eternal family and weaving his everlasting community behind the scenes: "You did not choose me but I chose you. And I appointed you to go and bear fruit, *fruit that will last*" (15:16)—fruit that grows amid the grit and grime of the everyday.

18
Talk About Love

IN LENT WE expect to hear about "being in the desert," but often such language sounds like a pious cliché. It helps to reinvigorate the imagery if some of us know real deserts at first hand, even better to have actually trekked through desert terrain on foot. In the days when I could still carry forty pounds on my back in the heat, I used to return as often as I could to the deserts of Utah, especially the Escalante wilderness.

This desert of red rock is not only one of the most beautiful places on earth, it is also a great teacher. The challenges of finding one's way, even with compasses and good maps, are formidable. You soon learn a lesson that is priceless for the practice of living itself: *You must expect to reach impasses and dead ends and to have to retrace your steps.* The desert is cruel-to-be-kind if you fancy that you will be able to make smooth progress. In the spring you can fall asleep under a starlit sky and wake up blanketed in snow. The deserts are deceptive; canyons are invisible from a distance and what looks like an easy way to a point on the horizon is barred by a precipice. The heat bends the light and tricks the eye. Distances are greater than they appear. You hit an impassable cliff; you have to turn around to find another way. The wilderness teaches you that encountering dead ends is part of life. (This assumes, of course, you aren't playing so safe that you've become a cruise passenger instead of a pilgrim.) The Spirit of truth is the enemy of our rationalizations. We do reach dead ends in our lives, in our work, in our relationships, in the ways we use our imagination to turn our lives into a story. And the Christ who emptied himself for us is the encourager of humility, keeping us company when we come clean with ourselves and others and admit: "I'm stuck here. I have to retreat from this cul-de-sac to find the new path forward."

If we learn this lesson, we will be less anxious about the dead ends we often reach together in the church. Impasses aren't the end of the world or the end of the church—just inevitable, and the clearest sign that the Spirit is instructing us to retrace our steps to a point from which we can set out afresh.

Today people are panicking because they think they have already reached an impasse over homosexuality, or because they suspect conversations between those who disagree will soon hit a wall. They are fearful, and decisions prompted by fear are unreliable, however justified by seemingly confident theologies. The action that is less fearful is to find the way back to the point where a new conversation can begin and go forward.

If we reach a dead end in controversy about the morality of certain physical expressions of intimacy, then God may be guiding us back to the more fundamental discussion we haven't yet been having—one we must explore if we are to break through to a better future in Christian witness about the graces found in intimacy, eros, and sexuality. I have a sense that we need first to enter what for many is virtually unexplored territory—the meaning of the *non-sexual* love that can flourish between men and between women. In fact, same-gender love is a vital and wonderful thread in the fabric of the lives of very many of us, quite regardless of our sexual orientation. Yet conventional Christian thought is strangely silent about the depths our friendships can reach, and intimate friendships are rarely held up for celebration in preaching or worship. Publicly, we show little awareness of the power that often makes the bonds of love between friends more enduring than vows of matrimony in a culture like ours, in which one marriage out of every two ends in divorce.

In leading retreats for men, I have discovered how powerful it is for us to share stories of friendship with other men and to testify how holy the need for male bonding is, how rooted in our souls. I think of a man—straight, happily married, a grandfather—who was able in the supportive circle of such a retreat to release over fifty years of pent-up grief over the loss of a wartime comrade whom he loved profoundly. I think of all the women who have confided to me how part of the secret of their fulfilled marriages was they hadn't expected their husbands to meet all their needs for intimacy, and so how vital intimate friendships with other women, sustained over decades, were for their well-being.

If Christians could retrace their steps from the dead end of flat disagreement about the moral status of homosexuality and talk more fully together about the deep love that can flourish between friends of the same gender, the spiritual climate of the sexuality debate could change for the better. Everyone can agree that God's Spirit is profoundly at work in the strong love of friends. Sharing this experience is the best preparation for exploring new territory—the possibility that the same Spirit is at work in the intimacy of committed same-gender partners who include sex among the ways they express their mutual love and dedication.

19
Sleepwalking

I FOUND MYSELF having to struggle at a party last week not to roll my eyes when someone discovered that I was a priest and immediately launched into a little speech about how they believed in *spirituality,* but no longer had any time for *religion.* This distinction between religion and spirituality has been popping up in casual conversation more and more in recent years. What does it mean? Was the person being merely defensive, using the distinction to fend me off? I am not sure, but if we are going to claim that spirituality and religion are alternatives or competitors we need to keep checking that the distinction is one that yields genuine insight.

One way of making the distinction is to think of religion as the sphere of *what*—what we practice as believers, what we believe and do. Religion is the collective sphere of our rituals and customs and observances and creeds. Religion is what we practice as members of a tribe or group with its own ethos, its mores, its calendar of observances. Spirituality is more the sphere of *why.* It concerns insight into our own unique personhood and the potential we have for an intimate relationship with the divine. Spirituality is about religion's soul and the risks of exploring the hidden roots of our behavior and values in our fears, wounds, and desires. In the realm of spirituality we don't content ourselves with learning the answers that our religion offers. We learn to ask for ourselves the questions those answers claim to address.

Does this distinction work? Well, we could try viewing the challenges of Lent through the lenses of religion and spirituality. Lent isn't too hard to go along with as a *religious* season. Purple or sackcloth vestments, serious preaching on moral issues, penitential atmosphere, a study group perhaps, temporary abstinence from a luxury—all valuable observances. But from the perspective of spirituality, Lent presents itself as the opportunity for personal soul-work. It could be a time for struggling with really fundamental questions of motivation and my own ambivalence about living close to God. Why is there so little freedom in my life? Why do I feel compelled to do so much of what I do? Why do I feel that so little of my behavior is a matter of free choice, good conscience, wise decision? From the standpoint of religion, Lent is the build-up to commemorating the historic event of Jesus' resurrection. From the standpoint of spirituality, Lent is a conscious process that, on the one hand, exposes our fear of being fully alive, our preference for a kind of sleepwalking, and on the other hand, resharpens our desire for the risen Christ to help us live with passion and awareness.

Lent as soulwork involves the commitment to examine ourselves, which has nothing to do with checking our lives against a list of sins, or spending hours raking through our so-called failings. True self-examination is about looking compassionately at what we do today and risking the question, "Why?" We look at what we are doing from day-to-day *now*. Not what we used to do; that's all over. Not what we might be doing in the future; we aren't there yet. With Jesus looking over our shoulder, encouraging and supporting, we ask the hard question: "Why?" We are simply seeking insight, not judging ourselves or feeling we have to make up excuses or explanations.

This year my self-examination is going to have several themes, all to do with freedom. I will sit in my chair with a pad of paper regularly and let insight gently emerge. One theme will be *repetition*. How much of what I am doing is simply repeating what I have done before? How many of my habits are actually out of date, pointless, or harmful? How might I do things differently in ways that match what is new in my life?

Another theme will be *conformity*. What do I do mainly because it gets approval from others, or ensures against their disapproval? How much of my behavior, when I look beneath the surface, is not at all an expression of my own creativity or gifts, but rather a performance to maintain the favor of others—some of whom are dead! And what about fashion? How much of my behavior is about letting current fads dictate my choices?

Another theme will deal with *addiction*. All of us in one way or another have compulsive patterns of behavior and, pathetically, we don't always get much pleasure out of the actual behaviors themselves. Often compulsive behavior is not necessarily clutching at a "high" but something we do to medicate or fend off feelings of sadness and emptiness. How much of my behavior is dictated not by the quest for rewards, let alone for creative achievement, but by the need to ward off uncomfortable feelings? I tend to overwork, but that overwork seldom derives from creativity in high gear. Instead, I feel I can't face the nasty withdrawal symptoms that well up when I stop—guilt and unease that spoil rest. Where is the freedom in this? Where is the freedom to accept Christ's invitation, "Come to me, all you that are weary and are carrying heavy burdens, and I will give you rest" (Matt. 11:28)?

Insight is not required to be religious, but it is the main quarry of spirituality. If I apply myself to gaining insight into the fears that constrain me, my desire to live differently can be aroused. "Sleeper, awake! Rise from the dead, and Christ will shine on you" (Eph. 5:14).

20
The Real Thing

I FOUND A loose thread in the sleeve of my jacket the other day and hesitated to pull it off in case it unraveled the entire seam. I did it anyway and of course the whole lining came apart. This made me think of certain questions we are reluctant to ask ourselves. We think twice about dealing with them in case we make a worse rip in the fabric of the story we tell about ourselves. Just now, as we approach the celebration of Easter, I am not sure that I want to ask: "How *real* will my Easter joy be this year?" Questions about the authenticity of our feelings scare us. Where might it lead if I start wondering whether my religious experience is fake?

So what is authentic Easter joy? Well, I do know it isn't relief at the return of spring, however welcome that is. Easter joy has to be something that I would experience just as much in the southern hemisphere, where Easter heralds the onset of winter cold. Easter joy is not a seasonal mood of uplift.

Neither is Easter joy to be confused with a sense that Jesus' resurrection is a reassuring illustration of the adage "All's well that ends well." A penetrating remark made by the fearless Anglican philosopher Donald McKinnon has always haunted me. He claimed that a lot of conventional talk about the resurrection misrepresented it as "a descent from the cross given greater dramatic effect by a thirty-six-hour postponement." The counterfeit version of Easter joy depends on the make-believe that God pulls a surprise "happy ending" on us after the ghastly setback of Jesus' crucifixion. Jesus is presented as a Houdini figure who, it seems, could not possibly have gotten out of the ultimate trap of crucifixion and burial in a sealed tomb. But no! To our relief—our so-called Easter joy—out he comes! All is well and our hero is victorious, the One they couldn't keep down! Happy Easter! Let's congratulate ourselves for being on the winning side!

Many of those who are skeptical about the story of the empty tomb and take the stories of Jesus' appearances as legends opt for an interpretation that is similarly reassuring. They assume the early disciples created the stories to express in a vivid but imaginary way their inner conviction that Jesus' soul had passed triumphantly and inevitably into heaven. But this is impossible to square with the evidence that the apostles regarded the resurrection as a shocking anomaly. Something utterly unprecedented had happened to transform the dead Jesus, and this transformation involved the passing of his body into an entirely new state. The visible trace of this transformation was an empty grave.

Easter joy focuses then on why God would do this unique thing to Jesus, something that by definition only he could do. If someone is raised while history is allowed to go on, this is God's only way of showing us what he is actually like. The resurrection is God's way of showing that it is the crucified Jesus who is the ultimate manifestation of his identity and character. In the resurrection, it is Jesus-on-the-cross who is confirmed as the "last word" about the nature of divine love and creativity—*and divine vulnerability.*

This is where it gets scary. The resurrection only makes sense as God's "showing his hand" about the meaning of the cross. So I can't have Easter joy if I don't find joy in Jesus-on-the-cross. In fact, I can't even believe in the resurrection, *unless I want to believe in a God who would be so crazy as to iden-*

tify himself with the crucified Jesus. God identifies with Jesus' choice to risk being crucified, his refusal to make the compromises that could have saved him from it. Paul speaks of the foolishness and weakness of God shown on the cross. The resurrection, far from supporting the notion of a triumphalistic deity of power, mysteriously confirms how deeply hidden and baffling the Creator truly is, as he reveals that he is at one with the man who so willingly exposed himself with an open heart to the fate devised by political power and religious expediency to crush him.

Authentic Easter joy—the genuine pearl of great price—is unfeigned delight in my heart of hearts that a hidden God turns out to be so different from all the stuff, aggressive or sentimental, that gets fabricated about him. Centuries ago, a custom grew up of beginning Easter sermons with a joke, known as the *risus paschalis.* The subtlety of Easter joy is like getting a joke. It is impossible to explain the resurrection to someone who doesn't get the foolishness of the cross. You either get it or you don't. The real God has authenticated himself in an event only the poor in spirit can appreciate. Easter faith comes with a desire to be in on the secret, to get the joke.

21
The Mirror of Pentecost

I HAVE A feeling that most parish churches prefer to keep the celebration of Pentecost as superficial and undemanding as possible. It seems to come and go without much thought, and some recent customs like encouraging the congregation to wear red and having a huge cake to celebrate "the church's birthday" look like mere diversions. I think, though, I have come up with a test that would show whether a parish was really ready to take Pentecost seriously. Is it prepared to ask regularly and boldly, "How is attention distributed and power exercised in this community?" Pentecost in the book of Acts is depicted as a shocking event that shows how God is restoring spiritual authority to those who are usually excluded from having any say. According to Luke, it made people think of Joel's prophecy:

> I will pour out my Spirit upon all flesh,
> and your sons and your daughters shall prophesy,
> and your young men shall see visions,
> and your old men shall dream dreams.
> Even upon my slaves, both men and women,
> in those days I will pour out my Spirit;
> and they shall prophesy. (Acts 2:17–18)

You could tell that the Spirit was shaping the church as a sign of God's hope for humanity by the way the community empowered each generation. Vision and authority weren't the prerogatives of one age group. The very young and the very old, and men and women whose inferior status kept them "seen but not heard" in society, were suddenly recognized as having powerful gifts, aspirations and challenges to offer this experimental new community.

Paul taught that the gift of the Spirit was a foretaste of what was ultimately in store for all of humanity. He used an everyday business term that meant a "down payment" or "first installment," and this helped to make those who listened to him realistic. They saw that *no* church can fully incarnate the new reality yet. But it could make a start and keep on struggling to realize as fully as possible this extraordinary goal of a community in which each generation is cherished, heard, and valued for its particular spiritual gifts and graces. And this is the continuing challenge that a parish today can take up if it wants to embrace its identity as a community of the Holy Spirit. One that refuses to look into the mirror of Pentecost is probably hiding the fact that one generational group, usually adults at some stage of middle age, is taking for granted its virtual monopoly of power.

Pentecost is a revealing mirror. The "miracle" was that each group of listeners from different cultures could hear the message in her or his native language. One gospel, but many different idioms and versions. One test for the maturity of a Christian congregation is to look for the opposite of the "one size fits all" mentality, especially in preaching and teaching. In a spiritually mature congregation there will be an eagerness to focus in turn on each of the generational groups that make up the whole. We will want to make sure that the good news can address in turn the issues typical of children, young adults, the middle aged, and the old.

Then there is another indicator of maturity. It's true that we have particular spiritual questions and concerns and opportunities that belong to each stage of our life. But we are often most in need of pastoral guidance and spiritual support during those crucial stages of transition when we pass from one phase to the next, like adolescence, the "forties crisis," that next critical stage in our fifties when we face our own aging and mortality, and then lastly when we face diminishment and prepare for the ultimate passage of death. A spiritually alive parish will be especially sensitive to meeting the needs of those who face the losses and gains and struggles of the hard "betwixt and between" times of life.

It is easy to misunderstand this emphasis on ministry that focuses on the particular needs of people at different stages in the life journey. "Surely," someone will protest, "if in our preaching or worship we regularly shift our focus and style to address in turn the cultures and needs of different age groups, won't a lot of the congregation frequently feel left out?" But humans are complex, and as we pass through each stage of life the issues, gifts, and wounds from the preceding stages remain with us. When the psychologists talk about our "inner child," for example, we can all grasp what they mean. During the whole of our lives we continue to deal with the fundamental needs that are most apparent in the lives of children. And in middle age we have to reencounter the dreams we had in youth. In growing up we often suppress our early ideals, and compromise with life. Later they return; the clouds roll away and we find in our fifties that the guiding stars we thought we had to ignore back then are shining down again.

We all need to hear the gospel in various idioms suited to the different generational needs. Isn't it common for adults to be deeply moved by a well-crafted sermon or service for children? Sometimes young people can be stimulated by teaching that a naïve observer would suppose to be way over their heads. Is it any wonder that the New Testament gives such emphasis on the Spirit as the giver, not of flashy "charismatic" gifts, but of complementarity and mutuality— training us not merely to accept but to revel in dependence on each other for fullness of life?

22

Praying in the Darkroom

"WHENEVER YOU PRAY, go into your room and shut the door and pray to your Father who is in secret; and your Father who sees in secret will reward you" (Matt. 6:6). I suppose Jesus' listeners shook their heads in puzzlement at Jesus instructions for prayer—they were to find privacy by going into a room where they could be in secret with God after shutting the door? Life then was utterly public and ordinary houses didn't afford privacy. He must have meant going into the toolshed on the roof or grainstore at the back. Rather eccentric. But Jesus was insistent. Our prayer isn't something other people can monitor or watch. In a world where we are constantly observed, supervised, and interfered with, prayer is an activity that is ours alone, where we "come into our own."

In my imagination, I associate Jesus' advice with my first experience years ago of developing photographic negatives in a darkroom. A neighbor gave me a battered old camera to take on my first trip abroad to Switzerland, and a friend who had access to the darkroom at school helped me develop my films when I returned. It made a deep impression on me in the faint reddish glow to see the image of the village church at Seewis appear mysteriously from nowhere in the chemical bath, and then to hang the photograph up to dry. Prayer for me is like that. We have to be patient and stay behind closed doors for a while for the process to "work." We bring to prayer our memories and images from scripture and worship that are usually as difficult to decipher as photographic negatives. But in the special conditions of the darkroom we can develop them, and the true images can emerge from the negatives.

I think of this particularly in the long season of the Sundays after Pentecost. It is as if the church recognizes that the religious intensity in which we live from Advent through Eastertide has given us more than enough images of God's presence and action in our lives. It is as if we have had a long session with the camera, taking in all sorts of pictures from Jesus' birth, his ministry, his death, and his resurrection. Now it is up to us to develop those images for ourselves. Perhaps we should give a warmer welcome to this long season of summer when the input from the Sunday liturgies is far less dramatic. The church is really saying "enough is enough," and giving us permission to take our spiritual rolls of film into the personal darkroom of our own prayer life.

Where to start? This year I find that I am long overdue to renew my own appreciation of the Holy Spirit. I have the equivalent of rolls of film containing images of the Spirit: images from hymns, passages of scripture and poetry, images from my own life experience in the last few months. But what good are they to me until I have developed them for myself in the darkroom of the heart?

I certainly need the time until Advent comes around again. I can hardly imagine getting through the process any sooner, given the variety of images through which the Spirit is revealed. I can do a quick inventory in advance of what I need to revisit and make my own all over again in the months ahead.

First, I'm going to listen to spontaneous promptings. For example, for days now a couple of lines from one of the old hymns to the Holy Spirit have been going through my mind: "What is rigid, gently bend; what is frozen, warmly tend." The Holy Spirit is God coming to us in our fearfulness of life. It is out of fear that we turn rigid. We recognize it in the church and the world: rigidity based on fear, usually rationalized as "standing firm." I recognize it in myself. I hold my breath. I stiffen. I rely on routines and set ideas. My rigidity is fearfulness of what is coming next. . . .

But also what is happening now. I will need to meditate on the imagery of God as life-giving Breath. Breath is the one thing we can't store up. I can't live off the breathing of ten years ago. I can't even live off the breathing of five minutes ago. I can only live from this breath now, and the same is true of my relationship with God, the Eternal Now. God is the now or nothing of my living. Only God-the-Spirit can train me to live the present moment, weaning me from clinging to the past, gently resisting my anxious straining into the future. I can only learn how to live now from the Now. "He breathed on them and said to them, 'Receive the Holy Spirit'" (John 20:22).

It is strange how the deepest lessons of religion are concealed in the most elemental of life's rhythms like eating and drinking and breathing. To learn again that our relationship with God is just like breathing itself is as simple as it gets, but it scares us. Loving God is repeatedly taking the risk of emptying ourselves and letting go of what has been, and then taking the risk of being receptive to the gift of what is new, like breathing in and breathing out.

Stars

23

Working Out

MY WORK AS a writer at the Holocaust Museum kept me sitting at a computer for most of the day, and so like millions of other sedentary workers I had to make "working out" part of my routine. When I first reluctantly started aerobics classes and working with a trainer, I was sure I would loathe it. During my years in a monastic order I used to get plenty of exercise outdoors helping to maintain the grounds and felt rather condescending whenever I glanced through the windows of the local gym at people throwing themselves around in the aerobics class or doggedly working on the machines. But now I get the point, and an exercise program has given me a fresh appreciation of the parallels between physical and spiritual exercise.

Historically, they have shared a common vocabulary. The word *asceticism* derives from the Greek word for physical training, and most spiritual traditions use basic expressions like "spiritual exercises," "spiritual disciplines," and "spiritual practice." Paul uses gymnastic metaphors when he talks about the process of spiritual maturation. This common vocabulary is no accident. Athletics and spirituality are both experiential, and their practices derive from age-old experience, now corroborated by scientific advances in physiology and our knowledge of the brain.

Spiritual tradition and the athletic arts both teach the importance of sheer repetition if we are to develop—and the importance of varied patterns of repetition to achieve balanced rather than lopsided development. We need routines. It would be useless for an individual to wander into a gym and do a few movements here, then one or two on this machine and that one, as impulse dictates. The results from such randomness would be negligible. Likewise, if we think we can grow spiritually by just praying whatever comes into our heads in the inspiration of the moment, we are heading for disappointment. Our brains and muscles, our imaginations and souls, require practice to develop, different patterns that are effective only by repetition—routines.

I have been thinking about this because in the last few months I have started praying Morning Prayer from the Book of Common Prayer before setting off for work. Now in talking about the daily offices of Morning and Evening Prayer I have to admit my experience is pretty extensive. I was educated as a teenager in the shadow of an English cathedral where the services were sung gloriously day in and day out. I attended these services at my Oxford college. I prayed them at seminary, in my parishes where they were part of the daily routine—and, of course, in a monastery for twenty-eight years. That's about as experienced as you can get. But when I recently embarked on the experiment of earning my living in a secular setting for a while and learning the ordinary rhythms of life as most people experience them, I didn't want to pray the Prayer Book offices at home by myself. Perhaps I just needed to discover whether I missed them or not. Eventually, I did. I am drawn back to the wisdom of the Prayer Book as a basic resource.

Praying Morning Prayer or Evening Prayer by oneself requires some getting used to, a bit like working out alone rather than in a class. The beauty and effectiveness of the daily offices is that they give us a work-out routine for our relationship with God. They help us repeat basics of prayer, relieving us of the need to make stuff up as we go along. The readings from scripture are found for us, the psalms allotted, the canticles prescribed, the prayers suggested, the collects that connect us with our Sunday worship set out.

Repetition causes all these spiritual influences to sink in over time subliminally. We don't have to worry about analyzing everything or trying to make every single line "meaningful." It is a spiritual routine—a word which from the world of physical training has the right to sound very positive. A routine that builds our health is not "mere" routine. Spiritual routines don't require us to have perfect attention; our minds wander but we know where to pick up again. Like physical workouts, they don't demand that we be "in the right mood": they are something we can do even if we got out on the wrong side of the bed.

The genius of Anglicanism is to have provided in the Book of Common Prayer for everyone, not just clergy, a compendium of worship that can work for individuals as well as communities, and can be used when we are in church or at home or on the road. We become a portable church when we take our Prayer Book with us. I will be packing my Prayer Book and Bible in carry-on luggage soon for a journey to see my family in New Zealand. Evening Prayer will be over the Grand Canyon. Compline at the gate at LAX airport. Morning Prayer over Fiji. Then the next Evening Prayer I will be watching the sunset on a pile of driftwood on Paraparaumu beach. And once I have settled in, I will report as usual to the Kapiti Gym so I can keep that other exercise program going, too.

24
Blank Pages

EVERY FEW WEEKS my mother sends me from New Zealand a fresh manuscript chapter of a memoir she is writing of her childhood so I can transcribe it on my computer. She had never dreamed of doing such a thing until my brother suggested it as a legacy for her grandchildren—and the great-grandchildren she is hoping for—who might want to know something of that distant life in an English north country village in the 1920s. But her sudden eagerness to tell her story stems, I'm sure, from something deeper than merely the good idea of a family legacy. As she negotiates her closing days, her childhood has laid claim to her. "How childhood tries to reach us," exclaims Rilke in one of his wonderful poems. She needs to tell these stories to round out her life just now. The stories are full of freshness and energy; they are so eloquent of her playfulness and vitality... and in the next installment she is going to deal with some terrible and painful times she is only just coming to terms with. Those need facing, too. It isn't a game.

There is an inner, spiritual work that can only be done by writing our life stories down. Last weekend I was visiting a friend who belongs to a women's spirituality group and I picked up a little booklet of short spiritual autobiographies they had written and collected. Simple as they were, each was a distinct achievement of insight and self-disclosure. Clearly this work of writing they had supported each other in had brought a tremendous blessing.

Sometimes, writing our story out is almost the only way forward. In my ministry I have helped many people write out for themselves the full life story of their own brokenness in preparation for making their first sacramental confession, and this led me to write my first book, *Reconciliation: Preparing for Confession in the Episcopal Church*. It is an incredible privilege as a priest to keep a sister or a brother company as they dismantle the survival apparatus of denial and self-justification and claim their identity as sinners sought by a wounded God. These are life stories that don't get told by daydreaming. They need telling out and writing down so we can hand them over to God, and tear up the pages after we have taken to heart the word of absolution.

The last time I wrote out my own story was in therapy. I had always been clever in telling a censored version of my life story that effectively banished suffering, that put a brave face on everything. My regular story was a pious blarney of interesting "achievements" and experiences. It took the piti-less discipline of psychotherapy in middle age to make me write out a hundred pages that for the very first time included all the unmentionable stories of abandonment and injury and resentment.

Writing a spiritual life story, though, doesn't have to be a response to crisis. And it is never about nostalgia or visiting the past for its own sake. We tell the past in order to bring us fully into the present. The adventure is learning that my story has never been just "my" story—what appears like my story is *and always has been from birth* "our" story, the story of Christ-in-me, me-in-Christ, Christ-with-me, me-with-Christ. It is not all about me, but about us. The pencil and paper, the laptop, is ours, and it is as if Christ is looking over my shoulder and encouraging me to tell my life stories in terms of the ups and downs and in and outs of our relation-ship. Times I was aware of divine company, and times when that was hidden from me. Times of discovery and times of loss. Times of growth and times of betrayal and unraveling. The pages are not all that important in themselves, but the process is. The product isn't a little book to feed reveries. We might seldom read it again. The most important result is when we arrive at today. By writing what has been, we arrive at the blank page of today. And the work of spiritual biography—telling our story as the history of a relationship with God in Christ—comes to fruition in the realization that the blank page of the now, the present moment, is an invitation to be co-creator of our lives with God. God hasn't fixed anything, and we are not taking dictation. We are not just "painting by numbers," filling in a preordained pattern.

Christ behind us, Christ supporting us tenderly, looking over our shoulder, is saying "What shall *we* make of today?" To be fully alive is to co-create—synergy—"working together with God" (2 Cor. 6:1), as the Eastern Orthodox saints loved to call it, taking their cue from scripture.

25
Meet the Gang

I WAS CLEARING out some storage boxes last week when I came across some old sheets of paper with some calligraphy exercises. How had these survived previous purges? I was a bit sad to remember the high hopes I once had set on calligraphy as my ideal pastime. I gave up after several months.

Most of us can remember setting out to learn a new skill like playing a musical instrument, painting, or a sport, only to give up before long because our first ungainly results humiliated and disappointed us. The muddy painting, the awful sounds, the clumsy movements are so different from the graceful creations of the experts we admire. In no time at all we have made up excuses to drop the project. We tell ourselves it just doesn't suit us and we didn't have the time for the new hobby after all.

Why do we give up praying—the kind of praying that takes time and going into one's room and shutting the door like Jesus said? Well, our first experiences of "praying in secret" are seldom what we want. We assume others who are praying in secret must be good at it, really focused in their conversation with God or serene in their meditation. In contrast, our experience is anything but focused and serene. What could be more discouraging than the whirl of distractions we experience when we try to speak to God and even more when we try to listen to God? Adept at lying to ourselves, it doesn't take long for us to come up with excuses for giving up the attempts to pray. Our temperaments are clearly not suited to this "inner stuff"; we are doers or extroverts. And it is a waste of precious time just to flounder around with all these wandering thoughts. We stuff down the shame of discovering that we are no good at prayer.

If we are lucky, a wise friend might see through our excuses and encourage us to start over. But her advice wouldn't be the same as she would give to encourage us to take up our sport or craft again. You can't say about praying, "Practice makes perfect; gradually you will get to be really good, so be patient with the messiness of your beginner's results. In time you will be proud of what you achieve." Instead, the advice might go something like this: "Look, prayer is God's way of getting you to meet the cast of characters you call your distractions. God knows we spend a lot of time disowning them and pretending we don't know them. They are *family*. Prayer will always be messy, because *they* are. Those 'distractions' are our mess; they're the mess we are in. So prayer is our rendezvous with them and God is present to introduce us." Maybe what we call our "distractions" are really the main event. Often God prefers to stay quietly in the background at first when we pray because the real business at hand is setting us free, and only truth sets us free.

Most of us are really bad at telling the truth, and we will never get better at it until we meet our preoccupations and obsessions, the stuff we are always telling ourselves deep down—only we don't realize it until we stop our activity. When we stop to pray, then these preoccupations swim to the surface and start splashing and jostling us. Meet the gang!

Instead of pushing them back down, arguing with them, cursing them, or trying to turn your back on them, why don't you try looking them in the face and treating them as parts of yourself clamoring for attention? The feelings they are revealing could be God's real agenda of prayer. The desires, resentments, memories, and messages that keep on insinuating themselves into your prayer might be the real signposts telling you what to pray about.

I bet your distractions are the "usual cast of characters." You try to pray, but you start obsessing about your "to do" list. Well, what a great opportunity to pray about the big lie you were probably told as a child about the importance of not being lazy, about being valuable only when you were meeting other people's needs, about the need to prove that you could stay on top of every situation. Your preoccupation is telling you about your bondage. So ask God about what it would be like to be free from this burden, free to take time out with a clear conscience. Ever drifted into a sexual fantasy in prayer? Did it embarrass you? A great opportunity to break a conventional taboo! Why not bring up "the big subject" with God and talk about what you are feeling about yourself as a sexual being just now, and ask God to give your sexuality a blessing today?

We don't always have friends who can be as frank as this but none of us has a better friend than the Holy Spirit to teach us about these encounters. Make a list of what seems to get *in the way of* your prayer, and ask the Spirit how these things might actually become *a way into* prayer.

26

Infatuation

A FRIEND WAS joking the other day about a couple my partner and I know who are in the throes of falling in love. He used the word *infatuation*, which always makes me feel a bit embarrassed. It reminds me of the mixed blessings of falling in love and the sense of foolishness that can come over us when the initial euphoria of attraction wears off. *Infatuation* comes from the same root as *fatuous*, and fatuous is what we feel in the letdown after the first flush of erotic love has subsided and we move on to weaving intimacy at a less exotic level. At least we can gain some comfort from the knowledge that we are not merely repeating a cultural script about the inevitable shortness of honeymoons. Science has uncovered an inherent sequence in the body's chemistry that is reflected in our experience. The sense of being unable to control the onset of infatuation or its fading reflects the fluctuation of different "love chemicals"—dopamine, norepinephrine, phenylethylamine and many more—in our bodies.

The script of infatuation is worth remembering when we consider typical patterns of religious experience. For many people their spiritual life is launched through an intense conversion experience or some kind of euphoric awareness of being loved by God. These can seem like true turning points and they can fill us with feelings of warmth, exhilaration, and purposefulness that can last for months.

There can be an onrush of fervor in which prayer seems easy. But then comes the letdown, when our fervor seems to evaporate, returning us to the normality we were used to before, or a disillusioning barrenness. Not all that different from couples who wake up some time in the first year of marriage to face the banality that seems to have replaced excitement.

A common reaction is to turn to religious stimulants in an attempt to recapture the earlier feelings. Evangelicals turn to yet another revival service. Those in the Catholic tradition might sign up for a retreat or Cursillo, or try a new form of prayer. Others fall prey to feelings of guilt—"I'm a worthless backslider"—or they take refuge in resentment: "God has let me down by abandoning me after a brief honeymoon." Others settle for a life of faithful Christian service and worship, and keep as a secret the fact that inside they don't feel devout at all and have ceased to expect any distinct religious experiences.

Many of the great spiritual classics deal with just this common story. The best teachers acknowledge the initial value of religious peak experiences as ways in which God seizes our imagination. But they are very aware of the risks associated with them. They know only too well that if we have all sorts of consoling and sweet and passionate feelings, we can begin to confuse them with God and start to be dependent on them. When we are deprived of the pleasure of those beautiful spiritual feelings, then we can respond with a melodrama of our own creation, and start resenting God for abandoning us. This resentment can fester as cynicism. Often the bitterest agnostics are those who used to be devout and committed Christians. Perhaps Jesus was alluding to this tragic reversal when he spoke about the vulnerability of some of those who have a deep spiritual awakening and healing only to be invaded by seven devils "worse than the first" (Luke 11:26).

The mystics teach us that God is responsible for weaning us off the early religious "highs." In spite of the stress of feeling so much less spiritual than we used to be and the disappointment that God no longer visits us in special moments of closeness and consolation and insight, the end of the honeymoon is for our good. It is an invitation to another stage of intimacy with God, a more mystical one. And by mystical they mean one marked by a deep intuition that God is in and around every experience, not just "religious" or "spiritual" experiences. The onset of a more mystical sense of God can only come when we give up identifying God with this or that special type of feeling or event. Then it dawns on us that God is not one of the actors in life's drama, entering the stage one minute only to exit again. Rather, it would be closer to the truth to think of God as the theater and even the play.

In *Behold the Spirit* Alan Watts uses the image of the mirror to suggest the difference between thinking of God as present only occasionally in special moments of uplift and inspiration, and the intuition of God as the ground and presence underlying all experiences without exception. As a mirror reflects all colors and shapes without interference,

> in the same way the mystical awareness of God does not contest place with other experiences and states of mind. Mental states such as joy, sorrow, exaltation, dejection, pleasure, and pain are as a rule mutually exclusive. But the mystical stage is inclusive, just as God and His love include the whole universe. There is no conflict between experiencing the Now and things which happen in the Now.

Losing our dependence on special religious experiences can open us to another perspective from which we can sense God as the presence which invisibly enfolds and contains all our experiences, however humdrum or vexing or beautiful or complicated or ordinary. We can stop expecting God to "get in our faces," and start to appreciate God as the mysterious Heart whose pulse beats below the surface in absolutely everything and everybody. If we "live and move and have our being" in God, to use one of scripture's most mystical expressions, then God is the ocean we are all swimming in, and there is nothing he isn't enveloping and sustaining. My religious experience is *all* my experience whenever I pay attention to its depth. The Spirit isn't present just in spiritual highpoints but in everything I live through in the now. Everything I experience is included: my boredom and exasperation and disappointment and longings; not just the rare and the special, but also the mundane and predictable.

27
Insidious Grace

I BOUGHT A new Daily Planner recently and have been filling it in with all sorts of schedules and notes. I suppose I was riding a wave of disgust at the degree of chaos in my life, wanting to impose more control on it. But something happened recently that reminded me how much of my life will never be under my control because God works with us through surprise and spontaneity, trickery and coincidence. I had been attending a regular discussion group and had decided to quit because I wasn't getting much out of it. But a friend prevailed on me to go with him just one more time and by sheer coincidence we met an old acquaintance in the parking lot of the church where the group meets, an old friend we had lost touch with who was now in serious need and whom we were in a good position to help. If I had stuck to my guns to keep my schedule under control as I wanted it, this connection would never have happened.

There is a tension in our lives between the honest desire to be purposeful and the neurotic need to be in control. When we want to control life in order to make it deliver what we want when we want it, we condemn ourselves to frustration after frustration and resentment permeates our days. Life resists our attempts to bend it to our own individual wishes and God won't play ball with our need to have everything fixed in our favor. We become "angry at God" for not arranging things in the ways our egos insist we are entitled. The opposite of this is resignation, going with the flow. If we can't control things we try to protect ourselves from disappointment by renouncing expectation, and we damp down desire. We will just take what comes with a shrug. But passivity is just as much a phony response to the challenge of living as the attempt to control things.

Life in the Spirit is neither of the above. God claims from us our purposeful engagement, our attentiveness, our intentionality. The gospel insists that our conscious engagement in God's creative process—our faith-in-action—is uncannily effective and real.

> The apostles said to the Lord, "Increase our faith!" The Lord replied, "If you had faith the size of a mustard seed, you could say to this mulberry tree, 'Be uprooted and planted in the sea,' and it would obey you." (Luke 17:5–6)

Yet this intentionality is not for forcing our individual wishes onto reality, but for opening ourselves through desire to its rich possibilities. It is active receptivity, hope expectant of underserved and surprising gifts.

One of the most common signs that we are discovering the world as a dance mysteriously charged with grace is that we start to honor coincidences in our lives, like my meeting with the friend in need in the parking lot. (And I have had far more unlikely encounters where the odds against their occurrence were astronomical.) Casual browsing in a bookstore in which I am merely passing the time in my lunch hour turns up a book that is exactly what I need to read now to speak to my deepest questions—a book that wouldn't have had any meaning for me before. An impulse to phone a friend I haven't spoken to in months, that leads me to connect with her in the very hour when she needed someone to talk to. An inexplicable urge makes a woman break her habit of keeping herself to herself in public spaces, and she starts talking to a complete stranger and—surprise, surprise—he says something really challenging that disturbs and provokes her so much that she can't help thinking of the biblical stories of meeting with angels. In the life of faith— intentional expectancy—coincidences start to occur much more often.

Our frequent so-called coincidences in which we sense the Spirit weaving connections help us build a private language with God. All intimate relationships create a private language that we can't really share with outsiders, and the secret signs we get from God through coincidences aren't always something meant to be shared with others. And it is not just a matter of shared language with God; it is also shared humor. The life of faith has its humorous side. God is playful with us, getting us to show up for opportunities of grace in ways that frankly seem like trickery! I remember wise words of Alan Watts from a book called *Beyond Theology:*

> It does not seem to have occurred to most Christians that the means of grace might include trickery—that in his care of souls the Lord might use placebos, jokes, shocks, deceptions and all kinds of indirect and surprising methods of outwitting men's wonderfully defended egocentricity.

I like my new planner, and I certainly need to stay organized, but I am thinking of inscribing a page at the front with a favorite quotation from a great soul, Charles Péguy. This poet and prophet had a deep intuitive understanding of the devious and spontaneous character of God's workings. "Grace is insidious. When it doesn't come from the right, it comes from the left. When it doesn't come straight, it comes bent, and when it doesn't come bent, it comes broken. When it doesn't come from above, it comes from below." Péguy's words help me pray to be both purposeful and open to the endless surprises of the Spirit.

28
A Spirituality of Shopping

IS THERE SUCH a thing as a spirituality of shopping? The question isn't facetious because there ought to be a spirituality for every activity. Religion doesn't consist in rare supernatural experiences, but it interprets all experience, exploring its depths. Spirituality allows the sense of God's presence in and with us in any activity, to become real to us through our imagination so that it evokes a response from our hearts.

Many of us have picked up the catch phrase "shopping therapy" to admit wryly to ourselves that sometimes shopping expeditions are inspired by other motives than the need to restock empty shelves. We often set out for the mall to seek healing. And that awareness is one way into the exploration of a spirituality of shopping. Spirituality is not meant to be an anxious scrupulosity that makes us second-guess our every move. But it is about the courage to take soundings in the deeper currents that flow beneath our everyday activities. What are the feelings that prompt us to seek the "therapeutic" benefits of shopping? What difference does it make to bring those feelings and needs into a conversation with God before we get our "fix"?

It is rather pathetic, but I tend to make up excuses to shop when I feel depressed or a bit trapped by routine. Making choices among the fantastic range of products in the stores gives a little boost to my self-esteem when no one else is feeding my ego. I secretly congratulate myself on my taste and my eye for a bargain, and feel rewarded.

When we are really prepared to sit with the needs that lie beneath feelings like these, and learn their meaning, we can begin to differentiate ourselves from our consumerist culture. And scripture helps us by naming and supporting that movement of differentiation in the words of Jesus recorded in the Sermon on the Mount. "Why do you worry about clothing?" he questions—and it is this anxiety that he asks them to explore. He straightforwardly identifies the anxiety that is preoccupied with food and clothing as typically pagan: "It is the Gentiles who strive for all these things." Yet Jesus isn't a fierce ascetic, for he assures his followers that "your heavenly Father knows that you need all these things." He sums the issue up with another question: "Is not life more than food, and the body more than clothing?" (Matt. 6:25–33).

Prayer explores these questions about our anxieties. What are we afraid that we lack? How unattractive do we feel? Experts in consumption offer their innumerable remedies in magazine features and television shows that range from innocuous style makeovers to extreme plastic surgery. Stuff done to us from outside, applied to the surfaces of our life to revitalize us. The experts often seem to admit that the secret is an interior one, and recommend their remedies as keys to inner well-being. But these insights exist in uneasy tension with the blatant consumerist emphasis on makeovers available for money.

In his Sermon on the Mount Jesus told his followers, "Consider the lilies of the field, how they grow; they neither toil nor spin, yet I tell you Solomon in all his glory was not clothed like one of these." These words evoke more inner skepticism than assent even among the devout, yet they define the focus for the kind of prayer that goes to the root of our susceptibility to the propaganda of consumerism. The kind of "makeover" of myself that I can get for money can bring a sense of well-being that frankly can seem more potent than anything I get from "going to church." Ralph Waldo Emerson wrote, "I have heard with admiring submission the experience of the lady who declared that the sense of being well-dressed gives a feeling of tranquillity which religion is powerless to bestow." The question is, what kind of religion is that? Spirituality is the practice that digs deeper to the possibilities of a profound inner healing that addresses the root anxiety about our lack of well-being.

Healing prayer means a willingness to face our anxious sense of lacking beauty and lacking worth in ourselves. It means a readiness to allow ourselves to accept the beauty that we have and embrace the worth that is intrinsic to us through our oneness with Christ. The lily does not toil or spin in a frantic quest to gild itself, and there's no need to manufacture or makeover something we already have—our beauty. The scriptures speak of being clothed with Christ. You cannot get more beautiful than we are already, only we don't realize it.

If you are prepared to seek inward healing through prayer, wanting to know your own beauty in the eyes of God, your own worth and richness in union with Christ, you are going to be a very different kind of shopper. Not driven; more likely to keep things simple and well-chosen. And as we grow more spiritually mature we become freer to let the things we wear and buy celebrate and express an inner fullness that even "Solomon in all his glory" didn't experience.

29
Making a Will

FINALLY, AFTER THREE years of foot-dragging, I am drawing up an entirely new will. Sometimes money is the only thing that talks to my obstinate soul, and eventually the only way I could stop procrastinating was to actually pay a lawyer the first half of the fee to force myself to get on with the paperwork. Now I find I have taken the plunge into an intense spiritual exercise which proves once more how true the saying is that God is in the details. It is all very well thinking in vague generalities about the end of one's life and the disposal of assets. But true spirituality is not a matter of abstractions. True spirituality generates the impetus to deal practically with what is concrete and real. I am having to picture to myself in meditation actual scenarios of my death, and even my dreams are playing their part in the process.

Filling in the questionnaires and lists I have been given is anything but a simple matter of ticking the boxes corresponding to obvious choices. Even though the questions about powers of attorney, living wills, and health proxies seem technical and formal, they are having a powerful effect on my imagination. For example, I have made myself picture my comatose body stretched out in the hospital bed after a calamity that has brought about the "vegetative state" we all dread. I am imagining my partner and friends taking in the doctor's verdict that would set in motion the decision to withhold further treatment and nutrition. I am trying to feel my way into sensing the emotional burden that they will have to bear if they have to enact the decisions I am now binding them to make.

Then there is the question of legacies. Am I stipulating certain legacies because I really want some of my money to help fuel movements I care about after I am dead? Am I tempted to include some causes merely because I don't want to be thought of as uncaring? Who or what do I want to recognize in gratitude? I thought it was going to be easier than this. I am having trouble weighing the sincerity of my values and need more time to think about particular people and communities to which my personal debt of gratitude is profound.

And what about my own funeral? I have officiated at the funerals of about a hundred and fifty people in over thirty-six years of ministry, from those of complete strangers to my own grandmother and my father. I suspect I have been retreating behind a certain professional familiarity to avoid imagining in detail how I want my surviving friends to celebrate my own passing from this life. Now as I get down to thinking about the final disposal of my body and the rituals that will surround it, the reality of my own mortality is hitting home.

Before I could finally commit the binding decision for cremation to paper I had to present to my mind's eye the picture of my own corpse being slid into the furnace, as I had seen happen to others. I had to picture the gray powder to which I will be reduced. I even found that a particular image of the container I wanted for my ashes came to my mind, and I realized that I could act on this choice now and ask a friend who is a potter to make it for me in readiness. And I have sat by the swimming pool at my apartment this summer with pencil and paper, the Book of Common Prayer, and the hymnal to choose the prayers and hymns I would like for the service. It seemed to me that this familiar setting would do just fine as the "still waters" beside which I could, in Christ's company, reckon with the reality that Fourth Street SW is, like every other address, situated in "the valley of the shadow of death." And if tears came to my eyes as I hummed the tunes of the much loved hymns with which I want my friends to bid me farewell, I could always take a quick dip to wash them away.

Every great spiritual tradition proposes meditation on one's own death as a necessity if one is to mature, and some of them prescribe specific and detailed spiritual exercises designed to challenge our natural fear and aversion. In a culture like ours that conspires to protect us from contemplating our own banal mortality while morbidly entertaining us with shows that sensationalize the violent deaths of others, the sober disciplines of thoughtfully preparing our last will and testament, living wills, and funeral arrangements might be the nearest equivalent to those traditional spiritual exercises. They are healthful spiritual tasks, to be done trusting that Christ is close by looking supportively over our shoulders.

30
Divine Discontent

WE CANNOT AVOID overhearing cell phone conversations anymore, and the other day I overheard a man vigorously accusing someone of wasting time in navel-gazing. I had to smile at the extraordinary longevity of this term of abuse. It was originally coined to poke fun at contemplative Christian monks who practiced yoga-like postures for meditation, including one in which they seemed to be focusing on their midriff. Here we are eight centuries later still using the expression to accuse people of unhealthy self-absorption. And you will still hear it used sometimes in the church to suggest that behind spiritual practices such as meditation and retreats lurks an unhealthy concern with self and a disconnection with the challenges of the "real world."

Unfortunately, some who recommend meditation fuel suspicions that prayer is motivated by escapism. "Contemplative" practices may be recommended as a soothing remedy for stress, and there is a romantic streak in certain circles that idealizes retreats as opportunities to enter a special devotional realm uncontaminated by the harsh realities of the everyday, and safe from the conflicts of politics. Fortunately for us there are others who take a different line, prophetic spiritual guides who insist that spirituality leads us into the core of our real stress, not away from it, and that it is intrinsically political.

The political realm is the sphere where it is very hard to know who is telling the truth, and to be a politically responsible human being is to engage with the hard work of *discernment*. Prophetic, biblical faith drives home the fact that human beings are masters of deception and self-deception, and that God insists we learn to tell the difference between truth and falsehood, sincerity and trickery, service and exploitation. We are urged to fulfill the painful, painstaking, never-ending task of shaping society through the truth—never-ending, because truth soon becomes a fugitive from the winning side in any regime change.

Jesus' practice of withdrawing for prayer is in seamless continuity with his prophetic mission to unmask the hypocrisy of those who claimed to be guides for the people, but were blind. Prayer deals with the disastrous results of blindness in the political realm of society and in the politics of our own souls. The hypocrites are not just "them"—that's the biggest lie of them all, and the commonest. We who are so adept at self-deception share in this blindness. Our motives are not obvious and they are seldom pure. To pray is to embark on the arduous task of learning with Christ to tell the difference between the truth of our own hearts indwelt by the Spirit, and the lies we tell ourselves to avoid facing who we are and what we are called to be and to do. The scriptures speak of Satan disguising himself as an angel of light, a mythic way of referring to the political dynamic of camouflage and deception that permeates all human societies and our own individual hearts, which are miniature versions of society.

It is simplistic to pray for guidance with the expectation that God will simply put a message into our heads about who to be and what to do, saving us from the trouble of doing the work of discernment. Praying is the work of "discernment of spirits," the work of paying attention to our impulses and dreams and fears, listening to them long enough and unfolding them painstakingly enough for us to recognize what is genuine and what is phony, and the difference between our heart's desire and the scheming of our ego.

Take discontentment. We have these feelings of dissatisfaction, voices that murmur "Surely, this can't be all there is? There must be more to this relationship, this job, this *life*?" We can smother these feelings or we can listen to them. We can risk sitting with them with God, and take the risk of asking what they mean. We don't know what they mean, and we can't look it up in a book. Prayer is taking the risk of finding a meaning that we hadn't bargained for, and might not necessarily welcome at first.

We might be surprised to discover through sitting in prayer that our inarticulate dissatisfaction is nothing less than the Spirit praying within us, subverting the status quo, probing us to hunger and thirst for fullness of life, getting us to extricate ourselves from compromise and shallowness. Our discontent is divine discontent, passion breaking through.

Or we might find out that our feelings of discontentment are the whining of the ego. I got up from my prayers yesterday with that discovery and it didn't fill me with shame. I just had to face that old insidious voice that likes to insist that I am entitled to constant fulfillment. Once I had given it a hearing, I soon began to feel the contentment that it had been suppressing, and I was reintroduced to my own deeper capacity to accept and be grateful for what I was being given today.

31
Rude Awakenings

ONE OF THE values of familiarizing ourselves with the spiritualities of other faiths is that they can hold up a mirror to our own Christian or Jewish traditions that are closer to home. Exploring strange territory by learning about other spiritual beliefs and practices, we return to scan our own familiar landscape with new eyes and see features we had overlooked.

Zen Buddhism incorporates shock tactics that are meant to jolt people. Here's a typical saying of a Zen master: "The Buddha is a bull-headed jail-keeper and the patriarchs are horse-faced old maids." To all appearances the teacher is committing sacrilege by insulting the Buddha and the sages of old. What is going on? Well, the teacher is driving home the point that conventional religiosity can become a prison, trapping us in unreality. Devotion to the Buddha as a perfect spiritual being, a hero on a totally different plane to the one on which we lowly mortals live, turns him into a jail-keeper rather than a liberator. It contradicts the emancipating message of the Buddha, which focuses on waking people up into actually realizing and accepting the one true "Buddha nature" that every single person already inherently possesses.

Through a lens like this we can bring into focus some of the dangers of religiosity in our own Christian tradition. We notice that Jesus, like the Zen masters, used rude awakenings. For example, he sternly challenged attempts to put him on a special pedestal as a kind of moral hero, brusquely refusing even the complimentary title "good Teacher": "Why do you call me good? No one is good but God alone" (Mark 10:18). He was vigilant to catch people assuming that there was a spiritual hierarchy: everyone had the potential to become equal members of one spiritual family. "And looking at those who sat around him, he said, 'Here are my mother and my brothers! Whoever does the will of God is my brother and sister and mother'" (Mark 3:34–35). And John's gospel emphasizes the potential each of us has to become intimates of God and his true offspring. Jesus teaches that the heart of each believer will become the place where God dwells, and that together his disciples will go on to accomplish far greater works than he himself achieved (John 14).

The thrust of challenges like these is to remind us of the tendency of religiosity to create a special class of objects of devotion, paragons of virtue in whose presence we can bask. But this devotion doesn't make much difference to us, except to turn us into devotees. In contrast, the good news is not about a special class of saints and heroes, but about all of us as we are. The good news is that you and I are Jesus' family and that you and I are intimates of God, sons and daughters of God, just as we are. The closeness of this intimacy creates the possibility that our lives and behavior will express the love that springs from it. By realizing that we and God are "family," we actually hear what God is saying to his beloved world and express it ourselves through who we are and what we do. What makes a Buddhist is not outward veneration of the Buddha, but an inner awakening to the revelation of her own true Buddha nature. What makes a Christian is not just worship of Christ, but inner acceptance of the gift of sharing in God's life with him, the enlightenment that we ourselves are "participants of the divine nature" (2 Peter 1:4).

Religiosity claims that the saints can help us here below because they are different from us. But in the new reality of God's grace, the saints help us by encouraging us to outgrow that illusion of a special spiritual aristocracy, leading us to realize that we all already possess intimacy with God as a gift and all we need to do is to realize who we are already. That is their secret, and the one they want to share with us.

This insight doesn't abolish our Christian celebration of those we call saints, but it alerts us to the real promise of an authentic relationship with them. Gospel-based devotion to Mary, for example, won't turn into a Madonna cult focused on miracles and apparitions. There is no greater miracle than the gift of intimacy with God and one of the greatest icons of that intimacy is the intimacy of mother and child, Mary and her son. Anglican devotion to Mary focuses on that miracle, and does so in a way that opens us to our participation in it. The more deeply we celebrate the beauty and the costs of that intimacy, the more we know about our own closeness to God, our own intimacy with Jesus. The deeper our devotion to Mother and Child, the deeper our own sense of what you and I already have, and who we already are.

32

Taking Notes

I WAS EDUCATED in the shadow of Worcester Cathedral in a school that Henry VIII created out of the monastic school that had existed there since Saxon times. History seemed very close. We could crawl through a coal cellar into the charnel house where the bones of Saxon monks were stored after their graves had been dug up in the Middle Ages to make room for the Lady Chapel. Another relic took us even further back into the Dark Ages. Viking pirates repeatedly raided the Priory. Eventually the monks captured a marauder, tanned his skin, and nailed it to the door of their library as a hideous deterrent to future raiders. After almost a thousand years, a large piece still remained on view in the cathedral. Repeated burglaries are very traumatic and can drive victims to take desperate measures. In the end, it was the library that the monks most wanted to protect, not the golden ornaments from the church. It was a matter of life and death for civilization itself. The passing on of the accumulated wisdom of the ages was in their hands. Anything thieves could take could be replaced—except the monastery's books.

I was musing about this recently as I considered how devastating it would be to lose the notebooks I have kept from my reading over the last four decades. Let me explain what they mean to me. I have always been aware that the impressions we receive while reading can be very fleeting, so I decided to adopt a remedy that goes back to ancient times. The Greeks and Romans thought of memory in terms of places in the mind in which data was stored thematically. (The Greek for place is *topos* and that's why we speak of "topics.") Disciplined readers memorized by copying down extracts from the books they read. The notebooks into which they copied the quotations were called "commonplace books" because they could always consult these notebooks to find apt quotations that had the same theme in common. The result was a copious or fluent style of speaking and writing. (From this usage, we get the English word "copy"; if you wanted to learn how to speak *copiously,* you needed first to *copy* down writing that had meant something to you.)

The trick is not to self-consciously "take notes" from a book, but simply to trust impulse and intuition. Whenever you read something that strikes you, copy it down in your own handwriting into a notebook exclusively dedicated to this purpose. Imagine a journal in which you don't write your own musings, but you do copy down quotations from any and every source as you read. Don't even analyze why you think it is striking. Don't censor yourself. Write one line or three pages, whatever it calls for. And don't be afraid to mix your sources up. I can open my notebooks and on two facing pages there might be a poem of Emily Dickinson, a graffito copied from an underpass wall, a few lines from a review of an exhibition of German drawings from a discarded newspaper I picked up in the train, a quotation from a Zen master, and some lines from one of Saint Augustine's sermons.

The act of copying these quotations *in your own handwriting* is a way of making them your own. In this labor of love, you are preparing them as ingredients in the recipes of your own soul work. This method soon reveals to us how active our soul is during our reading. At every stage of our life, month by month, our hearts and souls are hungry for nourishment and illumination. Subconsciously we know what we need, even if consciously we are not fully aware of it. So as we read—whether it is a novel, the Bible, the newspaper, a book on prayer—our hearts are scanning the pages more avidly than our conscious minds. When we have an "aha!" moment and conscientiously copy down the passage that has triggered it, we are responding to our own interior needs.

Now I can turn back to these notebooks and find all sorts of riches clustered together. In retrospect I can tell why they resonated at that time. See how I was struggling with the challenges of being emotionally honest; half the quotations I noted down at this time speak to that theme. In another time, I now realize how much my heart was picking up from my reading about loneliness, and at another about letting go. In some ways these notebooks throw more light on the unfolding of my inner life than any journal I might have written. And they keep alive in my memory literally hundreds and hundreds of books that I have read over the years, and enable me to feed again from their wisdom and pass it on to others.

I marvel at the tenacity with which the monks of the Dark Ages guarded their libraries so they could continue to hand on the legacy of ancient wisdom. I feel some kinship with them in keeping commonplace books, playing my own part in putting together resources of wisdom and insight for the journey of the soul.

33
Namaste

I WAS FEELING low the other day, the kind of time when one needs a surprise call from a friend; the phone didn't ring, though. Yet, after a while, I got the befriending visit I needed in my soul. Into my reverie of self-pity and confusion, a poem came back to me unannounced. In his poem "The Old Interior Angel" David Whyte evokes a scene from his days of trekking in the Himalayas. On the way to rejoining his companions, he arrives alone at a ravine where there was supposed to be a simple suspension bridge. To his horror he finds it in ruins: just a few cables with some fragments of planking "in a crazy jumble over the drop." However "young, male and immortal" he feels, he cannot risk the crossing. But just as he is about to turn back and retrace his steps, a little old woman bent under the weight of a basket full of dung arrives and greets him with the traditional salute *Namaste*—"I greet the God in you." Almost before he can reply, she swiftly passes on her way,

> and went straight across
> that shivering chaos
> of wood
> and broken steel
> in one movement.

The old woman represents that inner presence

with her no-nonsense
compassion
and her old secret

who is able to press on where heroes' courage falters. The
poem ends with the poet able to make the crossing after all:

"Namaste"
you say
and follow.

The poem takes us instantly into the paradox of the
gospel, the conundrum of the beatitudes of Jesus. What is
the secret of the crossing at which the strong balk, but the
poor in spirit can traverse in a single movement? What is this
"kingdom of God" that the rich cannot enter, but the hum-
ble can? I feel I must wrestle more deeply with this question
than I have ever done before. There is a crossing to make
which privilege, education, property, talent, influence,
insight, success—all those things so valued in our society, not
least in Washington, do not necessarily empower us to make.
Far from it. Instead, all these forms of wealth can have the
effect of freezing at the brink those who prize them, so that
they—we?—are inevitably "sent empty away," as Mary's
Song, the *Magnificat,* puts it in Luke's gospel.

It will be a long time before I really make progress in
grasping the paradox of the Beatitudes, but I feel that adoration is one of the clues. In my experience, it is the poor
who know best how to adore God. And in my experience,
it is the entitled and privileged who are most knotted up
with inhibitions to adoration. So much so that many have
absolutely no idea what it would be like. Privileged people
find it easier to *think* about God, and they may have *feelings*
about God and pray. Like crossing a ravine, adoration threatens to bring them into unknown territory on the other side,
and the affluent and privileged feel they just "can't go
there." As if to *adore* God were to mean entering some dan-

gerous emotional territory of spiritual surrender or dependence or vulnerability.

I suppose it really is all about loss of control. Wealth not only makes you feel in control, it makes you feel you only exist if you stay in control. And adoration is the antithesis of control. It is loving the Mystery we very inadequately call God *with the brakes off*. It is letting go of self, enjoying the Beloved for the Beloved's sake. "Loving without *why*," as the mystics call it.

If the poor have less to lose in their everyday lives, they are more practiced in having nothing to lose in their loving worship of God, in letting go, in admiring and revelling in God's "Godness." I have seen adoration clearly revealed in the faces of the poor. On the face of Norah, our Irish housekeeper, saying the rosary in her pew in St. Marie's. I have seen it in the faces of office workers in Paris who have come to church to spend half their lunch break in contemplation. I have seen it on faces radiant with song in backstreet parish churches in Wales. In Sri Lanka at wayside shrines. And, of course, since I'm not using the word "poor" only in a literal sense, I have seen it among middle-class churchgoers who have learned at no small cost to connect with their own inner human poverty, usually through meditation and the experience of suffering.

Loving the Holy One without why. Just because the Divine is absolutely to be loved with all one's heart. If God invited anything less, he wouldn't be God. Ask yourself a question: When I hear in church, "O Come, let us adore him," do I honestly know from experience what that means?

34
Prayer Rug

A RECENT TRIP to Morocco was full of wonders. Crossing the Atlas mountains through the snowbound passes. Tracing the necklace of oases down the valley of the Draa. Viewing the edge of the Sahara where the road ends south of Zagora. But I was also on a quest that led me to the *souk* at Essaouira on the old Barbary coast. I needed a rug. And I really mean *needed,* not just happened to want a decorative souvenir. So the stakes were high, as I sipped the rug merchant's tea, reviewing many possibilities until the one that was meant to be was spread out. Then, of course, the protracted comedy of bargaining began until both parties could settle. And now a small kilim Berber rug from a mountain village is glowing on my bedroom floor, an intense ruby red, with patterns of black and saffron.

I needed the rug because I have difficulty in settling down to pray. I always have had. Where to put myself? Where to face? How to sit? How to compose myself? When I was young I couldn't get orientated and didn't know how to "hunker down," as we say. Then soon after I was ordained, I went on a retreat. It began in a most peculiar way. The leader came to the front of the chapel and took off his shoes—his socks had holes—*and unfurled a small rug on the floor.* Stepping onto it, he produced a small bench and knelt down, slipping the bench over his ankles and settling back on it. Then he waved some yellowing sheets of paper and announced, "If you want a traditional retreat, I have five addresses here on the vision of Isaiah. Or if you prefer we could learn to meditate. Which is it going to be?" Alarmed and fascinated, we retreatants hesitantly agreed to forgo the five addresses and launch into the actual practice of prayer.

After that, I accepted the fact that I was prayer-challenged and needed all the help I could get—including a prayer mat. It proved to be the wisest of aids. The prayer rug that is a staple of Islamic and some Eastern traditions is a portable placement on the earth. It demarcates a sacred here-and-now. It strangely invites us to hunker down. The Greek mathematician Archimedes claimed that as long as he had a place to stand and a lever long enough he could move the earth. His claim has often been repeated because human beings are so aware that in order to achieve anything worthwhile we need a sense of place where we can orientate ourselves and stand fast. Nomads found the virtue of the prayer rug. If you travel, you can take it with you—a portable sacred space that wanderers can unfurl at any stopping place, whether those who once traveled by camel in the desert or those like us who crisscross a different kind of desert and end up in the antiseptic rooms of American chain hotels.

I paid the price for my forgetfulness. I couldn't quite find where to pray in the apartment. I tried here, I tried there. I couldn't settle. Eventually, I realized that I needed a prayer rug to create that sense of place. I had been mistaken in thinking it was something I had outgrown.

So now a patch of startling beauty greets me from my floor, made from the wool of sheep that have grazed the pastures of the Atlas. It is dyed with the stamens of the saffron crocus I saw growing in the little fields by mountain streams and with the bodies of insects that once buzzed around the meadows, and woven by patient fingers to timeless patterns handed on from mother and daughter over the ages. I take my shoes off before stepping onto it, of course. This is sacred ground. There is no bush burning, but the colors blaze, and the only power that God actually has is the power of beauty. Only the beauty of God can get us to stop what we are doing and stop what we are becoming while we are doing it. Moses was a very busy man, and only that burning beauty got his attention long enough to stop him in his tracks. My rug is helping God do the same for me.